Getting **through**

by John Meredith-Parry and Lorraine Weller

Edward Arnold

First published 1980
by Edward Arnold (Publishers) Ltd
41 Bedford Square, London WC1B 3DQ
Reprinted 1982

British Library Cataloguing in Publication Data

Meredith-Parry, John
Getting through.
1. English language – Text-books for foreigners
I. Title II. Weller, Lorraine
428'.2'4 PE1128

ISBN 0-7131-8013-7

Typesetting by Graphix,
Hounslow, Middlesex
Printed and bound in Great Britain by
Spottiswoode Ballantyne Ltd
Colchester and London

Contents

The book designed by Cliff Hopkinson
Drawings by Madeleine Bradbury
Photographs by John Meredith-Parry and Peter Weller

Acknowledgements

The publishers wish to thank the following for permission to reproduce copyright material:

British Rail for information adapted from 'How to choose your rail tickets' (30); Dickins & Jones for their sign (21); John Dickinson Stationery for Basildon Bond advertisements (49); Doncaster District Council for 'Ye Newe Map of Britain' from *Mental Maps* (50); Elliot Right Way Books for the European Map from 'Puzzles and teasers for the easy chair' (57); Fontana Books for the code from 'Free Time News' edited by Eva Wilson (8); General Election Co-ordinating Committee for Animal Protection for the poster 'Put animals into politics' (54); New Internationalist for material from 'The myth of childhood' (62); New Society and Paul Barker for the time map 'Britain's uneven shrinkage' from the issue dated 14th April 1966 (10); the following radio stations for permission to reproduce their logos (31): Association of Independent Radio Contractors, Beacon Radio, BRMB Radio, Capital Radio, City Radio, Radio Clyde, Downtown Radio, Radio Forth, Radio Hallam, London Broadcasting Company, Metro Radio, Radio Orwell, Pennine Radio, Piccadilly Radio, Plymouth Sound, Swansea Sound, Radio Tees, Thames Valley Broadcasting Ltd, Radio Trent, Radio Victory.

Figures in brackets indicate the pages on which the extracts appear.

Elementary section

LOOKING AROUND

Comparing costs

Look at these things.
How much do you think they cost?

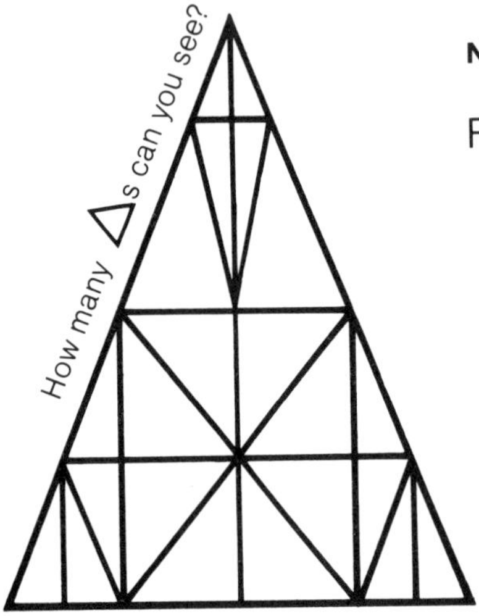

NAPIS = SPAIN What are the other countries?

RENFAC RUPE ANHIC KERMAND

IYLAT RAIN PYGTE LAVIYAGSOU

PAANJ SWEYTGNEARM

MUIBLEG CREEGE DENEWS

RUTIAAS DNALEAZWEN ZIARBL

XEMOCI OAOCMN TWAUKI

Family mealtimes

Which meal is this? What can you see on the table?

Saying 'Yes' and 'No' – politely!

Yes please

I'd love one / some

No thanks
I'm really full!

Would you like some more toast?
No thanks, but could I have another cup of coffee please?

LOOKING CLOSER

Differences

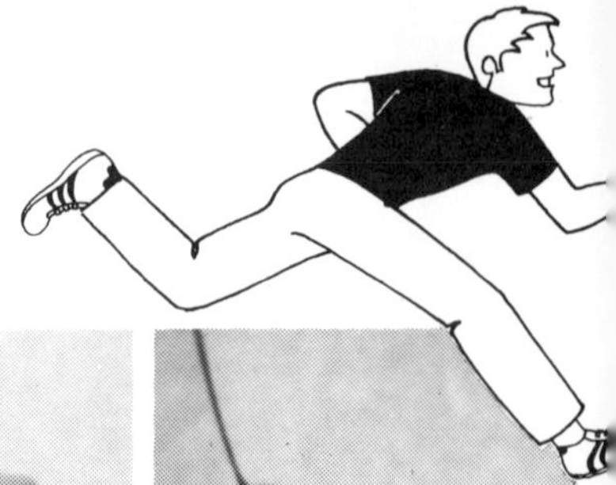

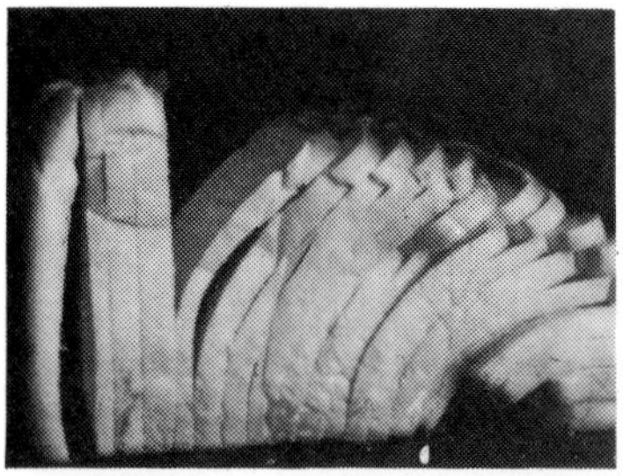

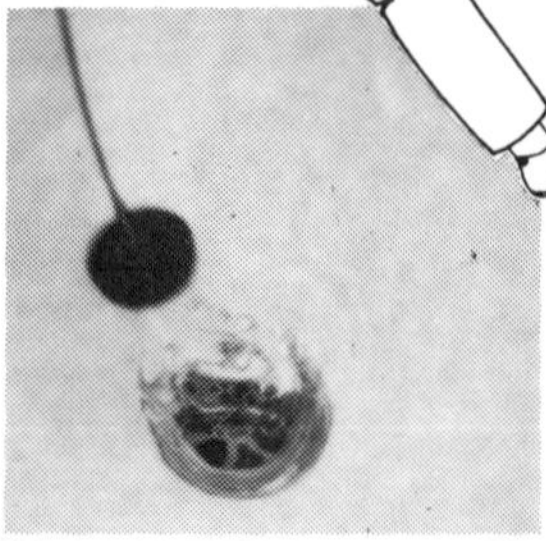

LOOK

at the photos. Can you make some sentences about Britain and your own country using these words?

coffee ... drive ...
eat ... plug ...
gardens ...
tea ... bread ...

Look at this code ...and work out the message.

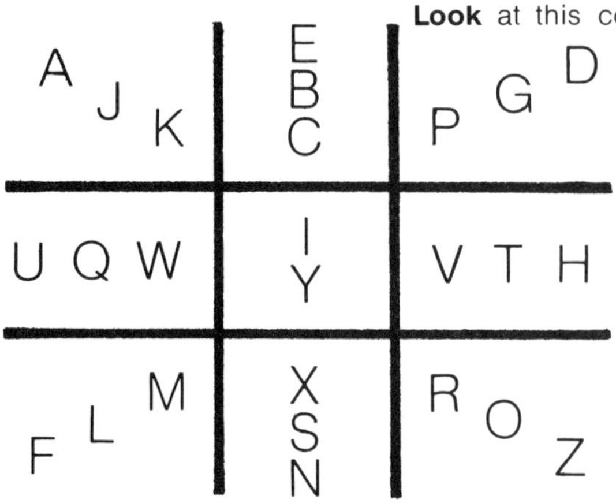

GETTING THROUGH

Phones and phoning

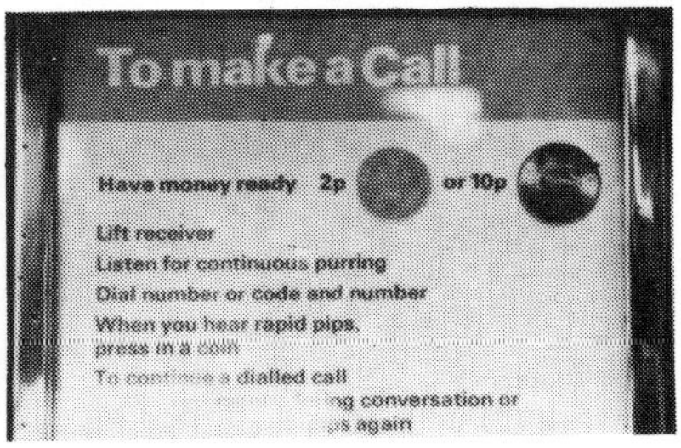

Can you work out these conversations?

It's Peter

Hold on a minute, I'll get her

Yes, who's calling?

Hello 6187

Hello, is Maria in please?

No, I'm afraid he went out about half an hour ago

O.K. I'll tell him

6187

I'm sorry I don't know

Yes, certainly

It's Sarah here, could you tell him I'll phone again tomorrow?

Thanks a lot, bye

Hello, is Nick in please?

Um...can I leave a message?

Oh, is he coming back tonight?

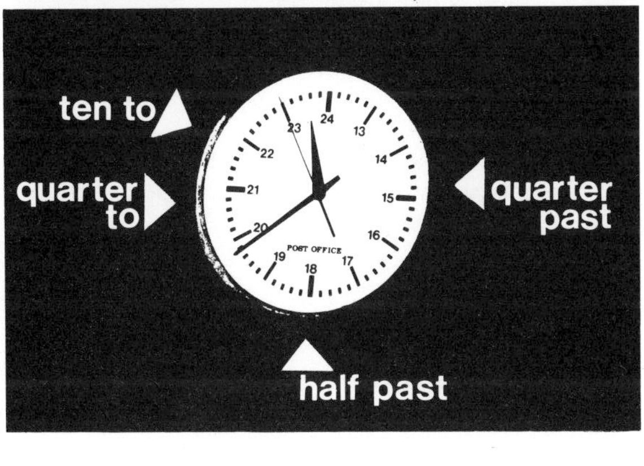

Distances and times

Map 1

Scale:
1cm to 160kms.

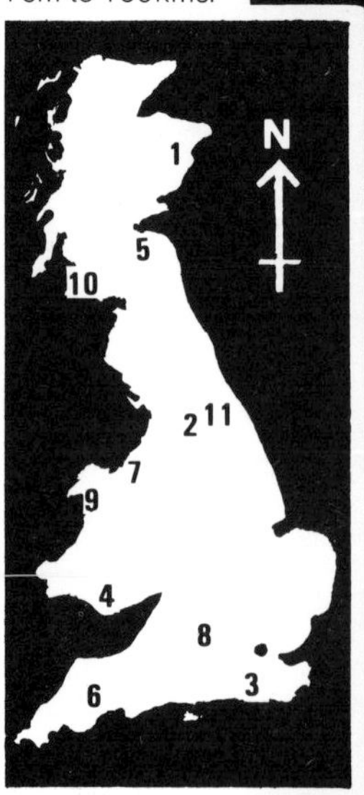

Map 2

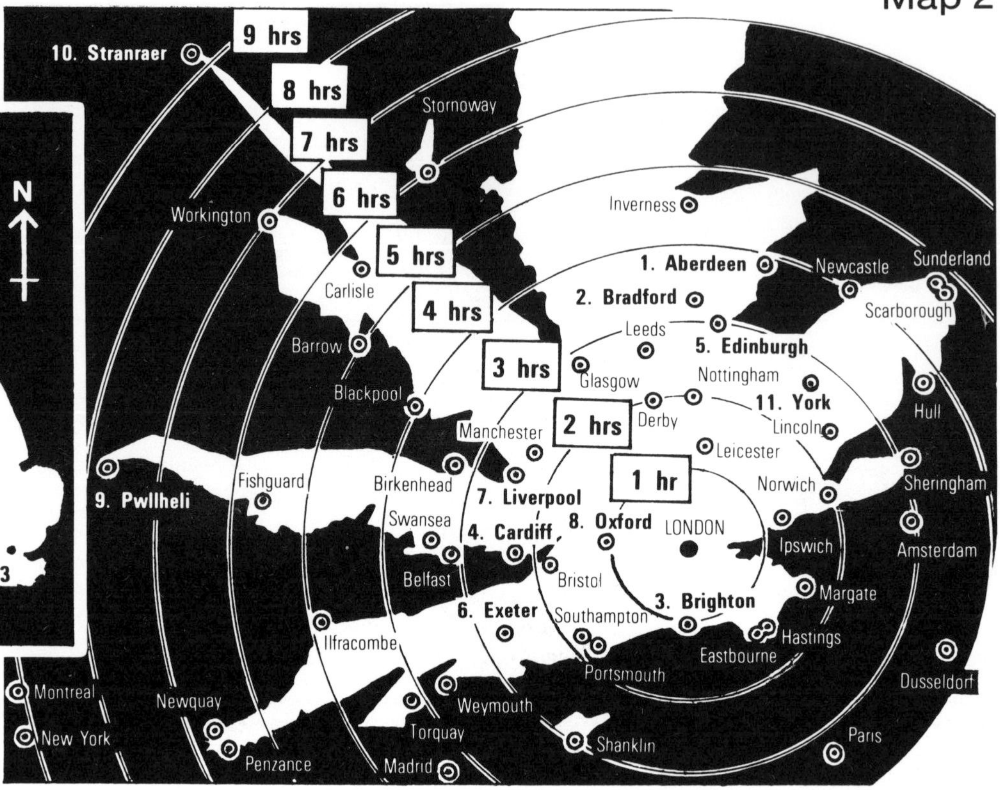

To change miles into kms, multiply by 8 and divide by 5. *E.g.*, from Brighton to Liverpool is 205 miles or 328 kms.

LOOK at MAP 1 and complete the sentences:

Edinburgh is about 645 kms north of London.
Cardiff.............................. London.
Oxford .... York.
Liverpool.......................... London.

Edinburgh is further from London than Oxford is.
Brighton is nearer to London than Norwich is.
Cardiff....... Liverpool....... Edinburgh is.
York .... Brighton .... Oxford is.

NOW LOOK at MAP 2

It takes three hours to get from London to York.
.... London to Edinburgh.

What do MAPS 1 and 2 show?

Look at MAP 2. What can you say about the travel connections between London and Wales, and London and Scotland?
Why do you think they are different?

Look at both maps and compare the following places:

Edinburgh/Bradford
Fishguard/Amsterdam
Pwllheli/Madrid
Oxford/Brighton
Paris/Aberdeen

Local papers

Under a Tenner

KITCHEN cabinet, 6ft x 3ft, £8. — Hailsham 842434.

STICKS of plumbers metal, £1 per 1lb stick. — Herstmonceux 2046.

WOODEN garden table, 48in long, 21in wide, very good condition, £3. — Herstmonceux 2046.

WARDROBE, 2ft 6in, £5. — Lewes 6778.

BEDSTEAD, 2ft 6in, wood ends with good clean mattress, £8. — Lewes 6778.

WHITE drop-side cot with mattress. £9. — Tel Seaford 890084.

TEN strong packing cartons, 5 cubic feet capacity, 50p each. — 2 Buckhurst Close, South Malling; callers pm weekdays.

YOU DRINK WE DRIVE
H. & H.
PRIVATE HIRE
061-761 6286 —p

Education & Tuition

ENGLISH for foreign students, full-time and part-time classes, examination courses, call in and see us. — Oakhurst School of English, 59 High Street, Lewes. Tel Lewes 71338.

Pick Your Own

Bramleys for storing 4p
Lord Lambournes 4p
Worcesters 4p
Laxtons for storing 4p
Coxs 8p
Cheaper for 30lbs
OPEN 9 to 7 daily
Pittlands Farm
Churn Lane, Horsmonden
Tel: Brenchley 2773

Opposite Brenchley Village Memorial Hall, take road one mile over crossroads to Castle Hill Stores, turn left down hill at De Claire Public House. Bear right at T road bottom of hill into Churn Lane (Marden Road). Carry on ¾ mile — Pittlands is second farm on left.

BUNN'S SECOND HAND DEALERS!!

Will buy your washers, fridges, cookers, display cabinets, bookcases, tables, dining suites, all kinds of furniture, cycles, prams, playpens, cots, stereos, record players etc. Full or part house clearances. For a quick pleasant deal:

RING "BUNN'S" — Day 764 8439. Evenings 764 6333. —z

BURY GROUP OF CHARITIES: Good as New Shop, 146 The Rock. Open Monday, Wednesday, Friday and Saturday. Goods required. — 764 2006. Will collect. —z

JUMBLE SALE at The Salvation Army, Moorgate, Friday, May 18th, at 6.30pm. (Jumble gratefully received on Wednesday, May 16th, between 2 to 3.30pm or 6.30 to 7.30pm).

Personal

UCKFIELD Town Council annual meeting, Town Hall, Tuesday, March 27, 7.30. TA31

SUICIDE? Despair? Telephone the Samaritans in confidence day or night. Eastbourne 35555. Hastings 436666. Tunbridge Wells 32323. TA36 m23

LOST & FOUND

LOST: Gold watch of sentimental value on the 8am 481 bus from Tottington to Bury on Saturday, May 12th. If found please ring 761 7184. —p

LOST: White budgie, Monday, May 14th. Fishpool area. — Tel: 764 0155.

British local newspapers give you useful information. Some are weekly and some are daily. They give you local news, tell you about local entertainments and have advertisements like these.

What's a tenner?

Draw a map to show someone how to get to Pittlands Farm from Brenchley Village Memorial Hall. Start like this:

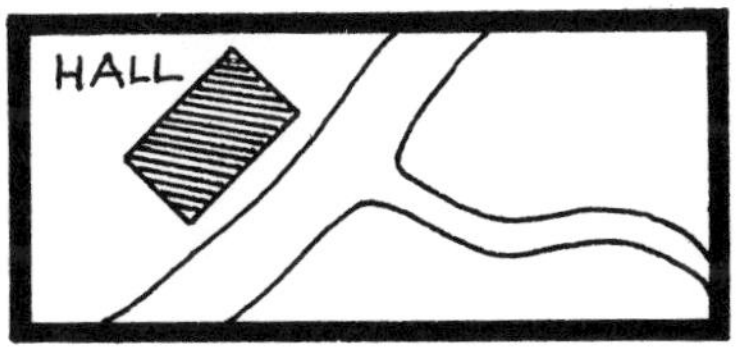

You want to sell a table and four chairs. Who do you ring?

You're going to a party. You want to have a good time and don't want to drive home. Who do you phone?

What happened on the 8.00am bus to Bury?

Who do the Samaritans help?

Who wants you to call in and see them?

SNAPSHOT SESSION

Photo-stories

Can you make a story by connecting at least *five* of these photos?

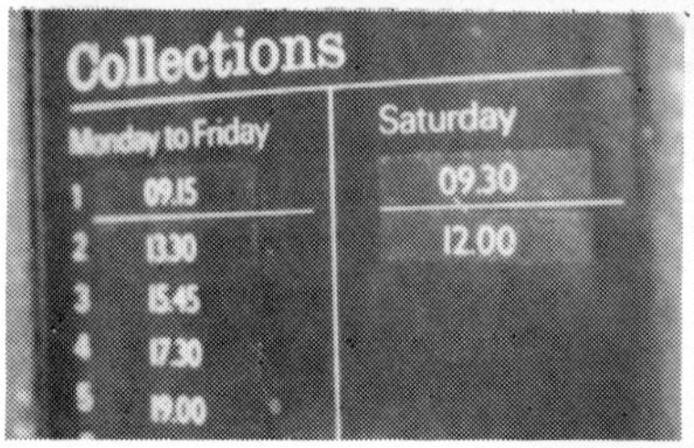

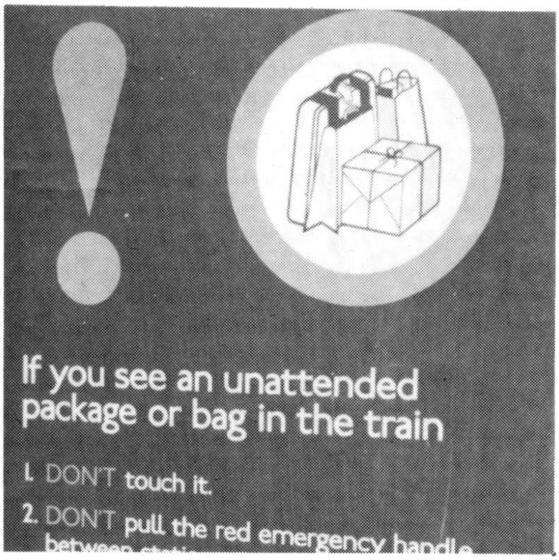

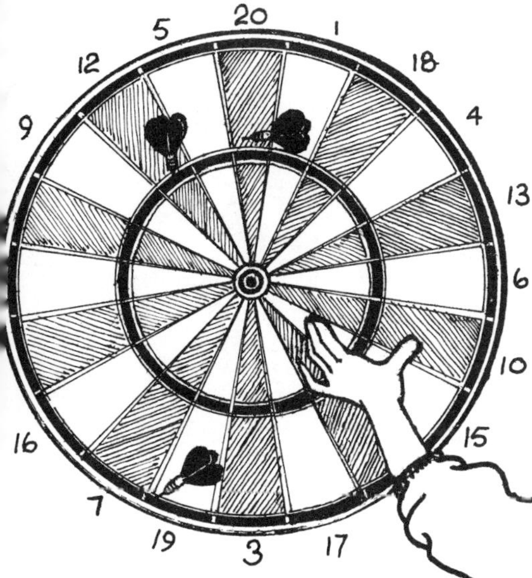

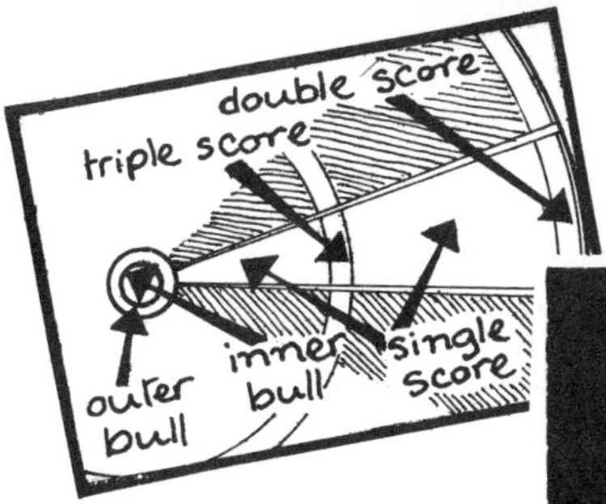

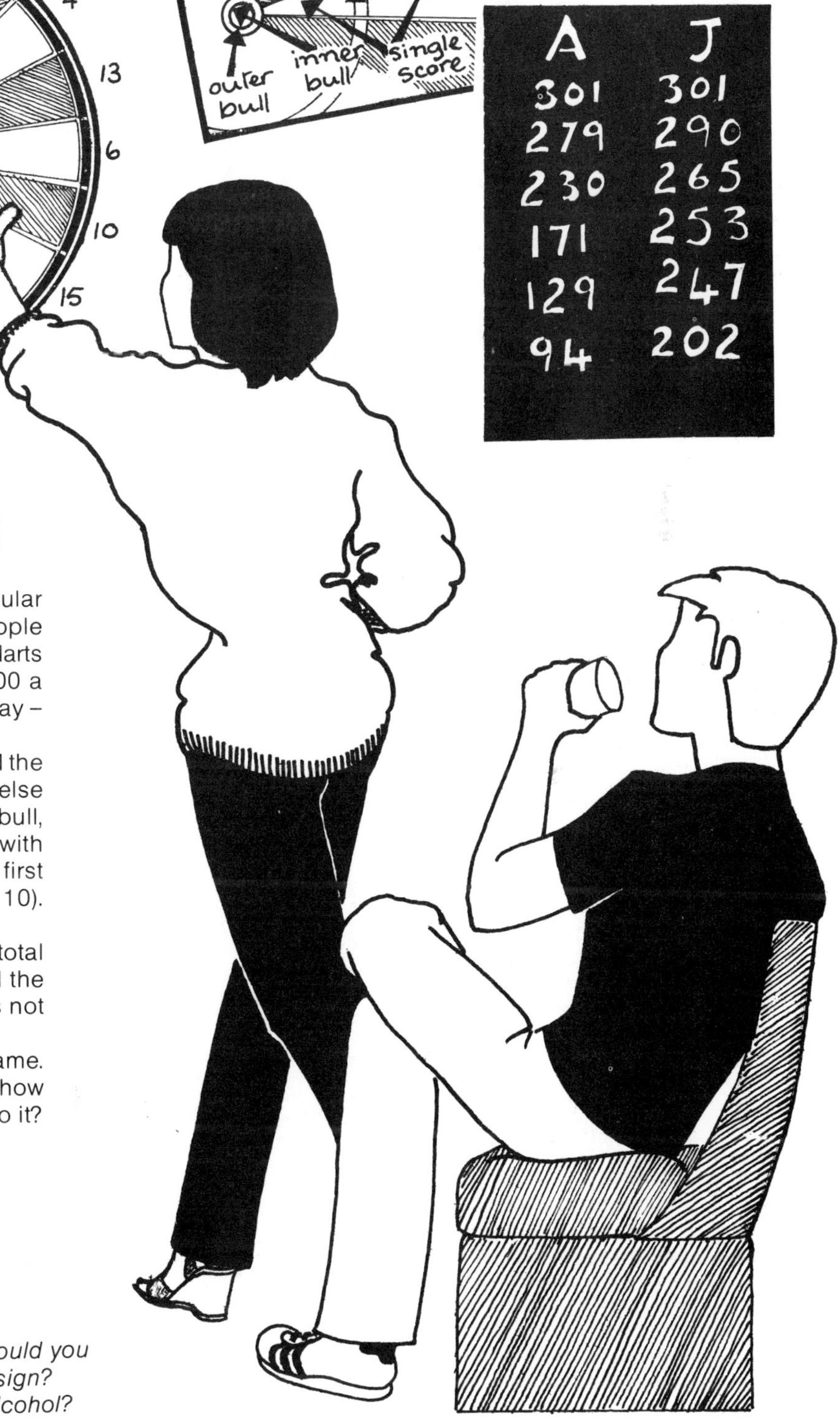

How to play darts

DARTS is Britain's most popular pub game. About 7 million people play every week. Professional darts players can earn up to £25,000 a year. It's an easy game to play – when you know the rules.

You have to begin and end the game with a double score, or else you can end on an inner bull, which scores 50. You start with 301 points. In this game, **A**'s first dart was a double 5 (total 10). Then she threw a 9 and a 3.

J started with a double 3 (total 6), then threw a 5. He missed the board with his third dart (he's not very good!).

A was the winner of the game. The darts on the board now show how she won. How did she do it?

Where would you see this sign? What's alcohol?

Who cares?

The British are so mad about animals that they started a society on 16 June 1824 to prevent cruelty to them. Today the society is called the RSPCA and is a household name. The first royal supporter of the society was the then Duchess of Kent in 1835.

At present, there are over 240 inspectors who:
investigate complaints about cruelty to animals;
inspect livestock markets where animals are sold for food;
give talks to schoolchildren;
painlessly put down animals that are old or sick.

The RSPCA helps 170,000 sick animals a year.
It puts down nearly 200,000 animals.
It also finds new homes for 43,000 unwanted dogs and 29,000 cats.

What do you think RSPCA means?
What do you think the society was called before 1835? What does "put down" mean here?
Can you give any examples of household names in your own country? What's "livestock"?
What kind of advice do you think RSPCA inspectors give to schoolchildren?

Who owns what pets?

Fifty per cent of British families own a pet. There are 5.3 million dogs in 4.5 million households, 4.6 million cats in 3.3 million households and 2.5 million budgies in 1.7 million households.

Every week, most people spend about £1.55 on food for their dogs. Cat owners spend about 98p.

There are four main socio-economic groups in Britain. The AB group earns the most and the DE group earns the least. Between them are two other groups: C1 and C2.

23% of the population are AB
15% of the population are C1
33% of the population are C2
28% of the population are DE

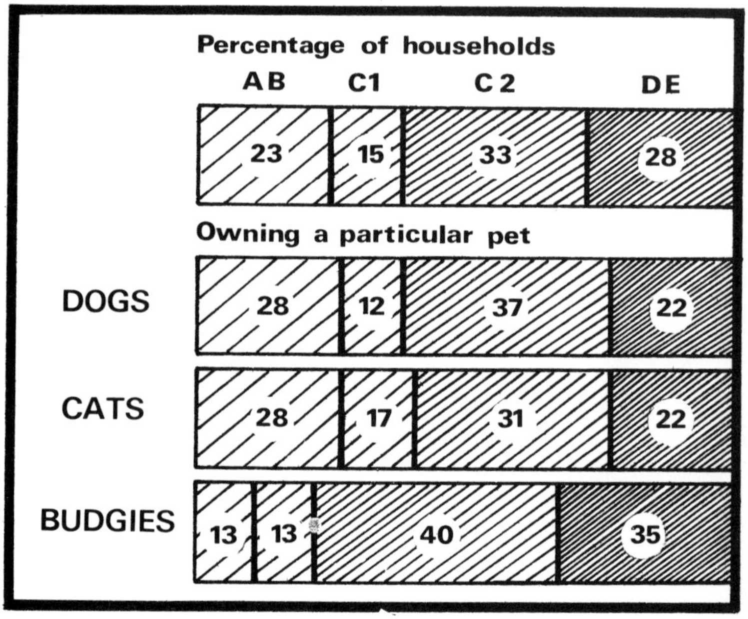

Look at this graph.

What does it tell you about:
C2 families
budgies
C1 families and dogs
DE families?

Tourists

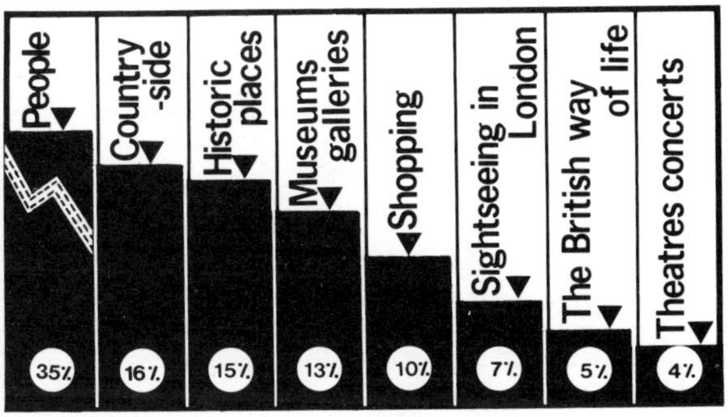

The British Tourist Authority asked some tourists "What did you enjoy most about Britain?" Here are their answers.

'People think that the British are cold and unfriendly, but that isn't true. They're very friendly and they're always ready to help.'

– Antonella Rita from Italy.

'Here in Britain, the weather is really very mad. One day it's all windy and rainy, and the next – it's sunny and warm. I never know what clothes to wear.'

– Ahmed Kamali from Iran.

'I love the way you British speak – it sounds so correct.'

– Bernie Brown from USA

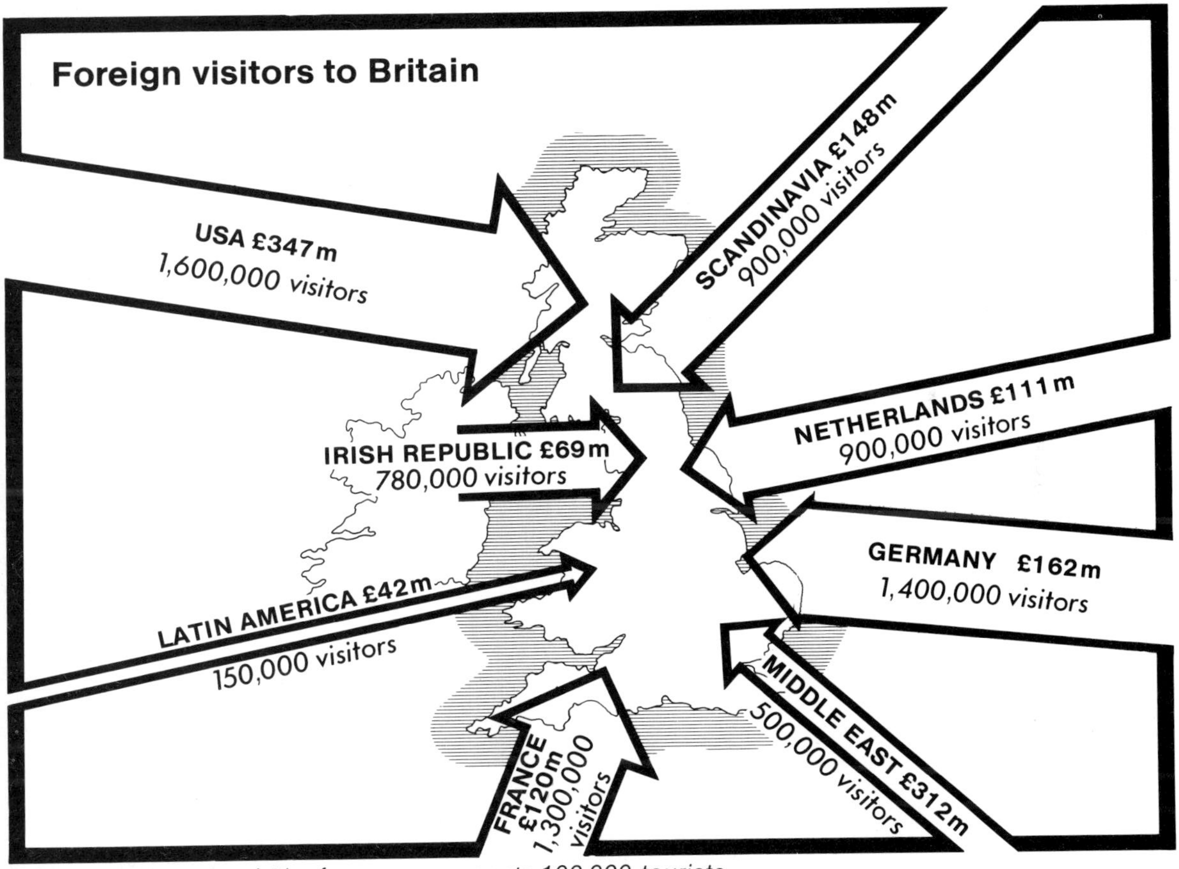

Scale: Each 1mm in width of arrows represents 100,000 tourists.

Look at this map.

Which nation brought the most money to Britain? What does this map tell you about Scandinavian and Dutch visitors to Britain?

How much did each visitor spend, on average, while in Britain? Give an answer for each nationality. Which nationality had the most money to spend? Which had the least?

Spot the Difference

Can you find 10 differences between the first drawing and the second?

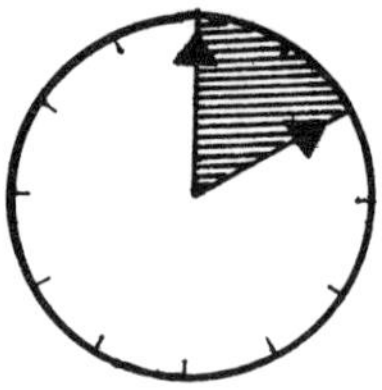

How many words can you make in ten minutes from:

MANCHESTER UNITED?

Birthday puzzle

The day before yesterday I asked Lorraine when her birthday was.

She said, "The day after tomorrow, I'll be able to say, 'yesterday was the day before my birthday'!" Typical author!

Could you sort it out for me? When *is* her birthday exactly?

Make connections

There's a dead man in a field. Next to him is an unopened parcel. Work out what happened by asking your teacher questions. Your teacher may answer only "yes" or "no".

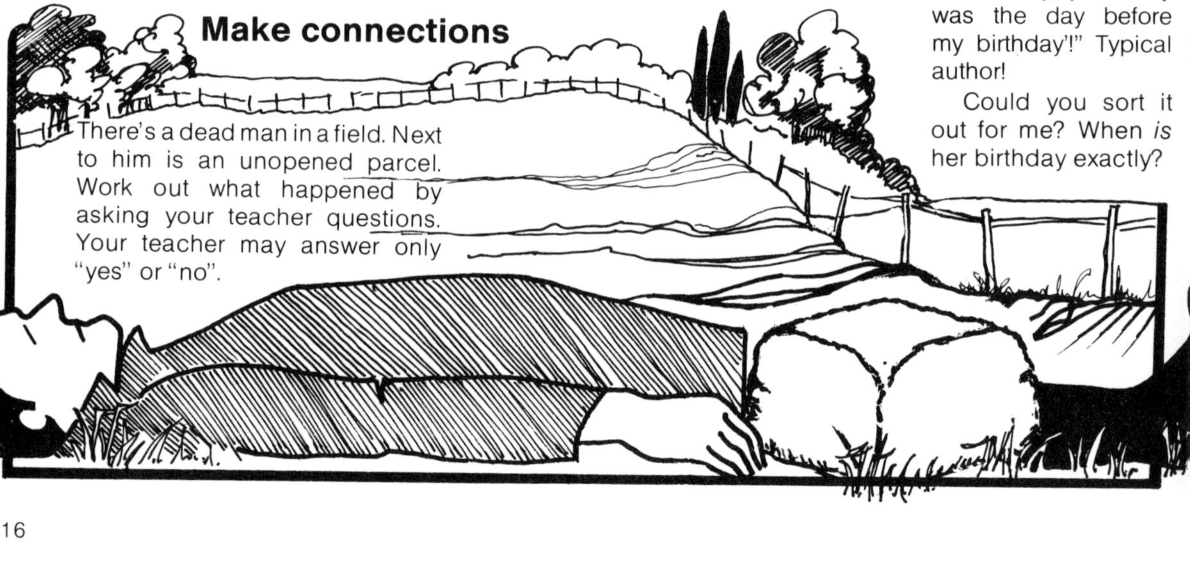

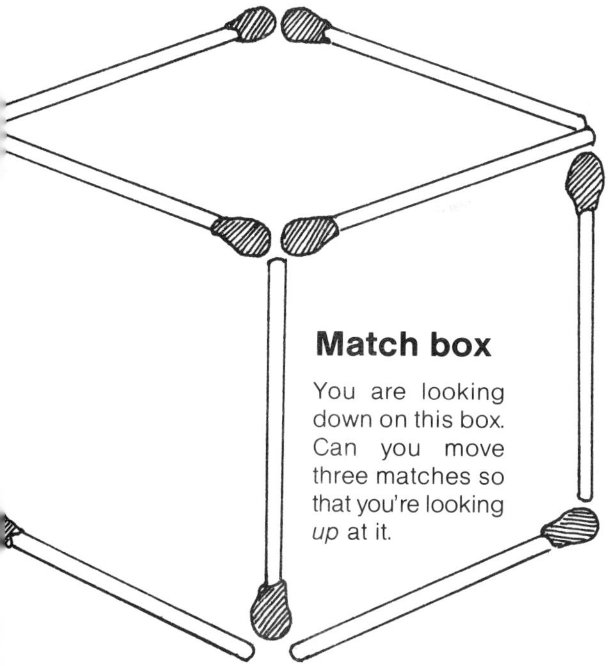

Match box

You are looking down on this box. Can you move three matches so that you're looking *up* at it.

Birthday numbers

1. Multiply the number of your birthday month by 100. *E.g.,* March is 300
2. Add the date of your birthday. *E.g.,* If your birthday is 24 September 1964, you add 24.
3. Multiply this by 2 and then add 8.
4. Multiply this number by 5 and add 4.
5. Multiply this number by 10 and add 4 again.
6. Add your age to this result and then subtract 444.

The answer gives the month and date of your birthday, and your age! The first number or numbers of your answer is the month. The next number or numbers is the date of your birthday. The last two numbers are your age! Clever, isn't it?

Can you do this?

(5) (10) (5) (10) (5) ← To go from this...

you have only five moves

...to get to this → (5) (5) (5) (10) (10)

A menu

VAT REG. NO 190-3250-85

PRICES INC VAT

To Begin

MACKEREL MOUSSE
A rich, creamy paté of mackerel, hardboiled eggs and gherkins 75p

THE CREAMY CRAB COCKTAIL
A Pelham Speciality 85p

HOME MADE PATÉ OF THE HOUSE 75p

SOUP OF THE DAY specially prepared by the Sussex Kitchen 40p

A COCKTAIL of mixed orange and grapefruit 60p

PRAWN COCKTAIL 75p

Continuing

CASSEROLE OF CHICKEN
Cooked in a cauldron with red wine, olives and mushrooms and including a selection of vegetables £2.20

SUSSEX FISH DISHES
Scampi & gougons of Sole, deep fried golden, served with petit pois, French fried potatoes, tartare sauce £2.60

ESCALOPE OF VEAL
Fried in butter, herbs & garlic served with a selection of vegetables £2.60

THE PELHAM PIE Steak and kidney, homemade, served in a rich, dark sauce and including vegetables £2.10p

PRIME FILLET STEAK grilled to your choice and served with a selection of vegetables £3.85

TOSSED GREEN SALAD 40p

SPECIAL DISH tonight:- see table card

To follow

PELHAM POT O'CHOCOLATE 65p

A selection of ICE CREAM or SORBETS 55p

VANILLA ICE CREAM with chocolate or butterscotch sauce 65p

HOMEMADE MERINGUE and fresh cream 70p

SYLLABUB 70p

Selection from the CHEESE BOARD with French bread, biscuits and butter 65p

Cona Coffee 25p black or with cream. Cover charge to include bread & butter 15p
Service NOT included, excepting parties of 5 or more when 10% may be added

WINE LIST OVERLEAF

What's the name of this restaurant?
Can you think of other words for "to begin" "to continue", "to follow"?
How many home-made things can you see here?
What are they? Who made them?
The name "French fried potatoes" is American. What do we usually call these potatoes in England?
Where's the wine list?

INTO THE EIGHTIES

Computers

The newest industry in Britain is micro-electronics and computers. It is growing very quickly. 25 years ago, most computers weighed about 3 tonnes and cost about £100,000. Today the same computer weighs less than a kilo and costs £150.

This is all because of the micro-processor which carries electronic messages on a thin piece of silicon. You can see how small it is in the photo.

People often think that computers are clever but all they know is the difference between 1 and 0. It is the computer programmer who uses this fact to make the computer do different jobs. Today a computer can do 100 million calculations in ONE SECOND. We already use micro-processors in our everyday lives *(below)*.

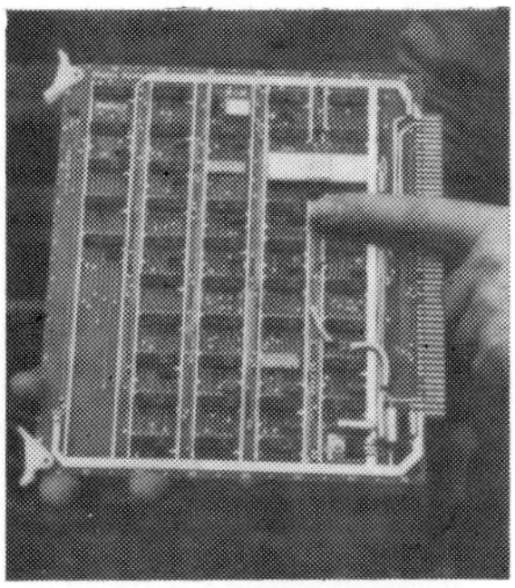

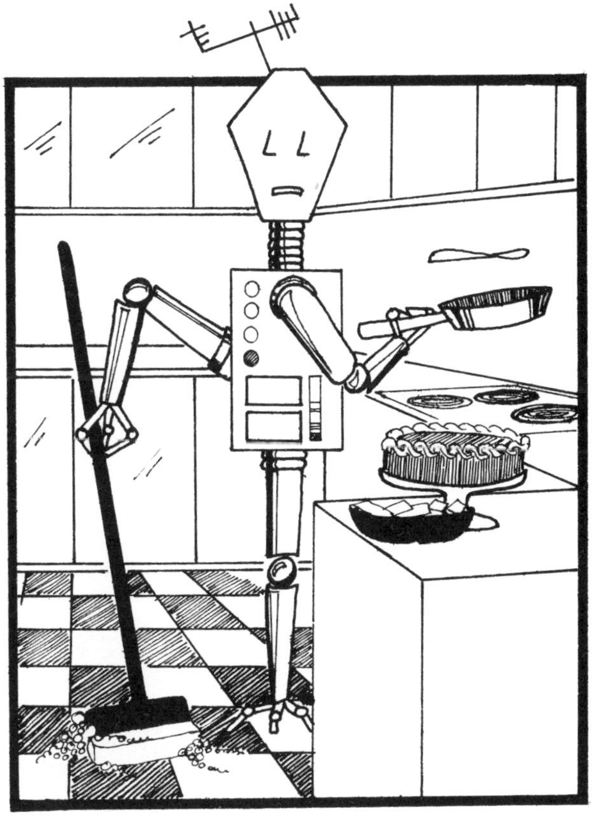

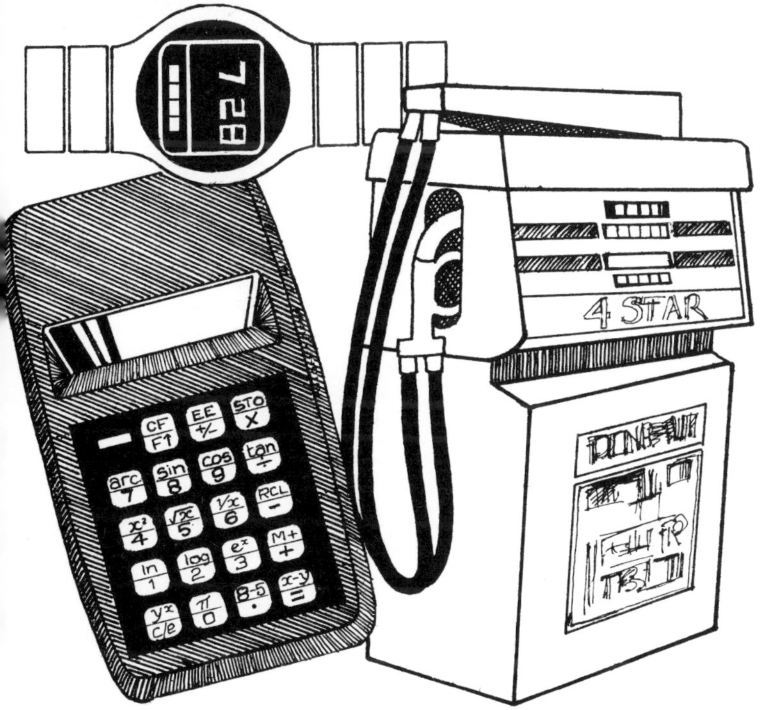

But computers are doing other things....

Did you know that:
In America, you can buy a robot for £2000. It cleans floors, mows lawns and does simple cooking;

in the American Prairies there are driverless tractors to cut the wheat;

in a town called Tama, near Tokyo, they have TV sets that print newspapers in your own home;

In Britain, a computer called Muppet can translate 50 words from English to French and vice versa.

OUT AND ABOUT IN LONDON

Travelling around

Here are some pictures showing things that tourists often do in London. These pages are to help you read and understand signs which you will see in the city. Imagine you are in London yourself. Look at the pictures and answer the questions.

1. Many tourists have difficulties when they buy an Underground ticket. They often have to queue because they haven't got any change for the machines. So always carry 5p and 10p coins.

But there are other difficulties for the poor tourist. Look at what you have to do to buy a ticket from a machine and to get to the trains.

Can you put the photos in order and give easy instructions to anyone who doesn't know the underground?

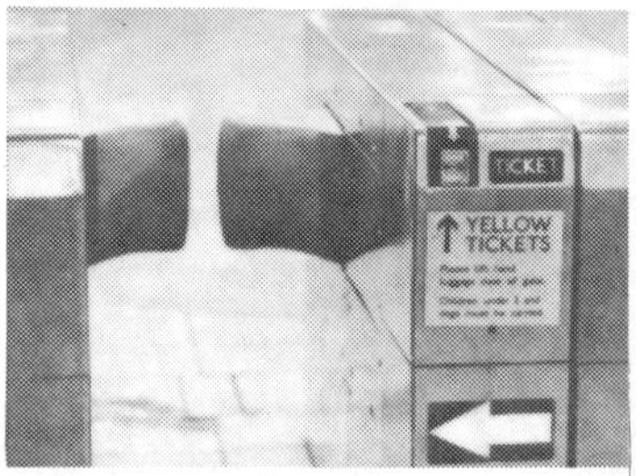

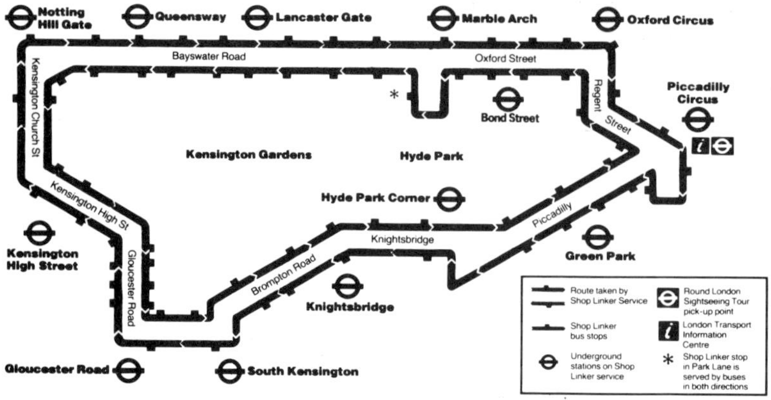

2. *This special bus (above) helps tourists. Where does it go to?*

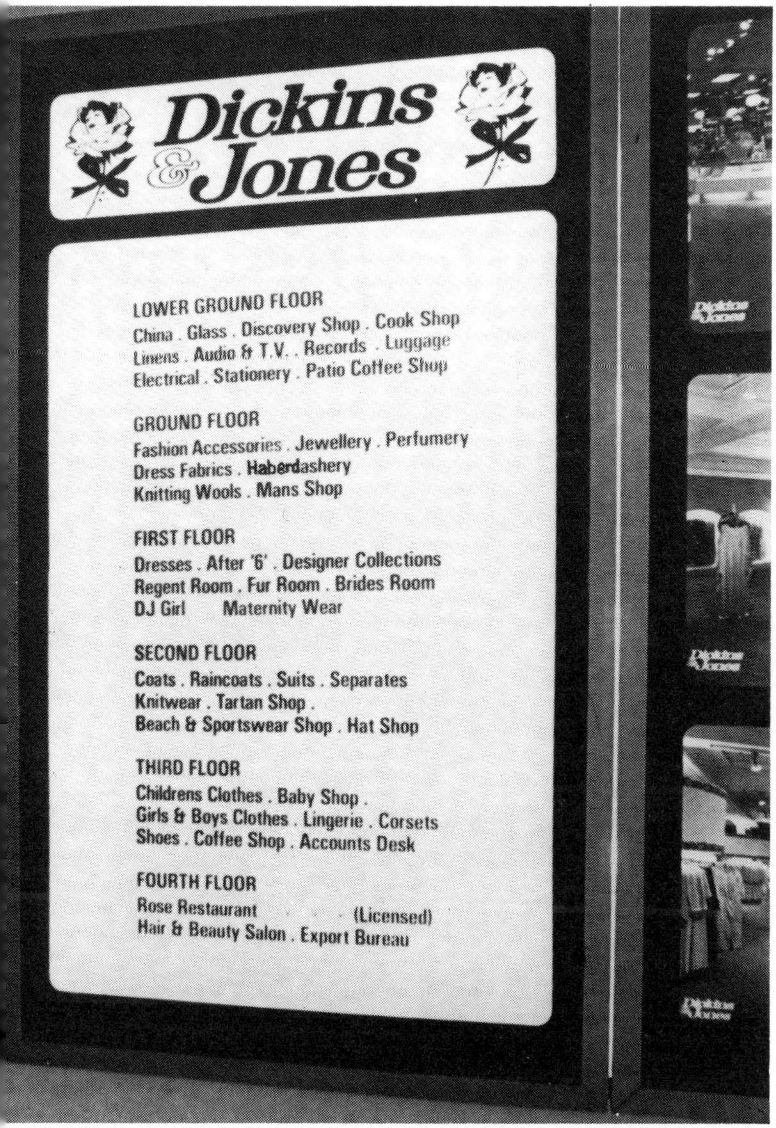

3. You take the bus and get off at Dickins and Jones. Look at this list of presents you want to buy for friends and relations at home.

a) Which floor and which department do you have to go to if you want to buy:

a Scottish kilt
a cassette recorder
a nightie
writing-paper
a cashmere sweater
a brooch
a souvenir tea-towel
swimming-trunks
a book of English recipes
a teapot.

b) You decide you need to sit down and have a good lunch and a glass of wine. Which floor do you go to?

4. After lunch you want to go sightseeing. You decide to go to the Tower of London but you're not sure that this is the right bus. What do you ask the conductor?

West End Cinemas

ABC 1 & 2 (QUEENSWAY) BAYSWATER.
1: EVERY WHICH WAY BUT LOOSE (AA)
2.40, 5.20, 7.55. Late show Fri & Sat 11.15.
2: SUPERMAN (A)
1.45, 4.25, 7.35. Late show Fri & Sat 11.15.

ABC EDGWARE ROAD.
SUPERMAN (A)
2.00, 5.10, 8.20. Progs 1.25, 4.35, 7.45. Late show Fri & Sat 11.15

ABC 1, 2, 3, 4 & 5 FULHAM ROAD.
SEATS BKBLE LAST SEP PERF. (Doors open 15 mins prior) Licensed Bar
1: SUPERMAN (A)
1.45, 4.40. Sep perf 8.15.

5. After your busy day, you decide to go to a film. You buy a paper and choose *Superman*. You know it's a popular film but you don't want to queue. You want to book in advance and arrange to meet a friend at the cinema for a drink before the film starts.

a) Which cinema do you choose?

b) When is the earliest time you can have a drink in the cinema?

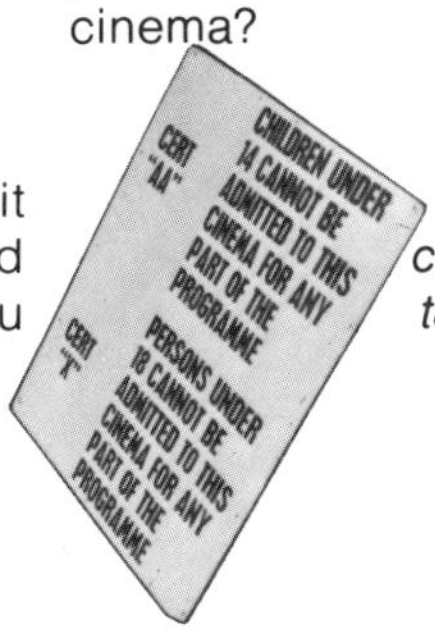

6. *If* **Every Which Way But Loose** *were on at this cinema, could you take a 13-year-old to see it?*

Annabel Evemy – schoolgirl

What age-group does your school take, Annabel?

Er...11 to 16 in the main school and 17 to 18-year-olds from next year.

Your school's called a Community College. Could you explain that?

Well, it just means that it's for everybody in the village to use, not just 11 to 18-year-olds. In fact, my mother studied sociology with the fifth form a couple of years ago.

Really, how did she get on?

Oh, she loved it, she got her O level! The school's open in the evenings as well, mostly for Adult Education classes...they learn all kinds of things: yoga, pottery, woodwork, local history. Some of the subjects are really interesting.

I always hated wearing school uniform when I was at school. Do you have to wear one?

Oh yes, the school's very strict about that...they think it makes us all look the same, so you can't tell which kids have well-off parents.

D'you think that's a good idea?

Yes, it's a good *idea*, but in fact, if they let us wear what we wanted, I'm sure we'd all wear jeans...

And what about other school rules – are there a lot of them?

No, not really, but the stupidest one is about smoking. If boys ge caught, they have to pick up litte in the school-yard. But if you're girl, they send a letter home to you parents.

And you don't think that's fair?

No, it's really unfair...they shoul do the same to all of us.

Is it the same in your lessons: d the boys study different things?

No, we all do woodwork an metalwork and art and – er cookery, plus things like Englis and Maths up to the age of 14 Obviously – after that – people ca choose.

What are your favourite subjects

Oh, French and German – definitely

Why's that?

Well, I enjoy learning languages. love going abroad in the holiday – on exchange visits. I'm sure learn more in a week abroad tha in a year at school!

Really. How?

Just by speaking the language All we do at school is lear grammar. We never say anythin and the teachers always speak i English – actually, we don't thin they can speak anything else!

You're probably right... But on th whole, do you like school?

Most of the time...yes!

LOOKING AHEAD

Reading tea leaves

All foreigners know that the British spend most of their time drinking tea. There are three reasons for this: firstly, we're a thirsty nation; secondly, we don't know how to make coffee; and thirdly, we believe we can read the future in the tea leaves at the bottom of our empty cups.

This explains why the traditional British "cuppa" is never made with teabags. So, put the kettle on and relax! We're going to reveal the secret world of the British tea-drinker...

When you finish your cup of tea, empty it into the saucer and, keeping the cup upside down, turn it round three times clockwise.

Now you need the expert skills of the teacup reader who looks for signs in the patterns in your cup.

Imagine you're reading your friend's teacup. The first things to look for are "tears". Take the cup from your friend and look to see if any tea is running down the inside. Sometimes there are a lot of "tears", sometimes only a few, and sometimes none at all. What do you think they mean?

Next you must try to see patterns in the cup. Here are some of the most usual ones: question-marks, bridges, roads and hills. All these things mean future problems for your friend.

Spiders are very bad news: tell your friend that someone she likes will disappoint her. After that, she won't want to be friends with that person.

Look for initials in the cup: they can tell you more about the problems. Ask your friend if she knows anyone whose name begins with any of the letters you can see.

You don't just want to look for bad news, so look carefully into the cup. Can you see a bird flying near the edge? This means good news from abroad will come soon. Lots of birds can mean foreign travel in the near future.

Don't forget to look for these if you're both going home soon – she'll be astonished at your intelligence!

Tiny tea-leaves, which look like dust, scattered around the cup mean that your friend will get some money soon. The more there are, the more money she'll get.

Finally, if you can see a hammer, this is very good because it shows that your friend will have success in something that's very important to her.

Look carefully at the cup shown here. Can you read the secrets in it? Change what you **see** into what you **say** about the future.

MAKE AND TAKE HOME

Badges and fudge

How to make "Ye Olde Englishe Fudge"

You need: 225g butter, 1kg sugar, a large tin of condensed milk, a cup of ordinary milk, vanilla essence, a saucepan with a heavy bottom.

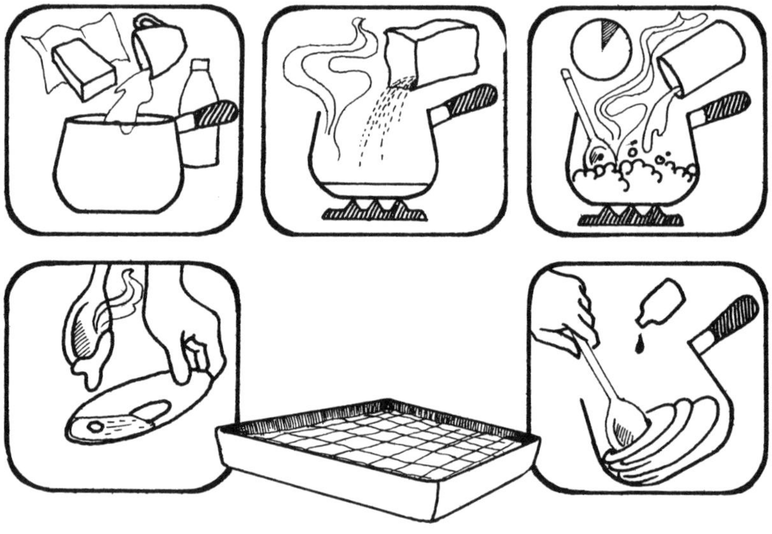

First melt the butter and the ordinary milk in the saucepan.
Add the sugar and let it dissolve slowly.
After that, boil for five minutes, stirring all the time.
Add the condensed milk and boil everything for about another 15 minutes.
Take a small amount of the boiling fudge and put it into a saucer of cold water.
If it stays soft in the water, it's ready.
Then remove from the heat, add the vanilla and beat with a wooden spoon for two or three minutes.
Pour into a dish and leave to cool.
Cut into small pieces to take home.

Make to how a badge British

Empty it

Keep it flat with a wooden spoon

Keep the heat very low

Watch carefully – things happen fast

Take a crisp or a peanut packet

As it gets smaller, keep turning the bag over

Or use some glue to fix the pin to the back

Make it flat and put it under an electric or gas grill

When the bag is the size you want, remove it from the grill

Put a safety-pin through the back of the badge while it's still warm.

Intermediate section

Comparing costs and services

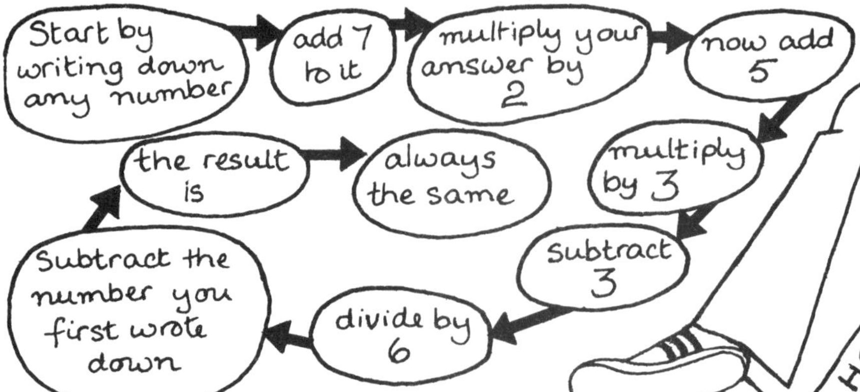

GETTING TOGETHER

Families

People used to work very long hours but nowadays families have much more spare time. We asked people what they did in their free time. Most of them had more than one interest! *(See chart below).*

Family free time

Public holidays in England:

New Year's Day
Good Friday
Easter Monday
May Day
Spring Bank Holiday
August Bank Holiday
Christmas Day
Boxing Day

How many public holidays are there in your country?

Most European countries have more than Britain. Why do you think this is?

Can you make complete sentences from these statistics?

Interview another student and make a similar chart to show the amount of time spent on spare time activities.

As only 29 per cent eat regularly in restaurants, you can see that most English people eat at home. When you stay with an English family, you'll probably like most of the food you eat but sometimes, you'll want to say "no"! Here are some ways to say "no" *politely* when somebody offers you something you don't want or don't like.

I won't thanks... I'm putting on weight.
I'm on a diet.
I'm trying to lose weight.

Thanks very much but... I'm not really keen on...
I'm not very fond of...

But sometimes this isn't enough and some people will continue to offer you food. In this case, 'Really, I couldn't" is a nice way to refuse a second time.

Use the new language to finish the dialogue. Here's the situation:

Mrs. Williams loves to see people eat. You're staying with her and you're on a diet. You've already lost ten pounds and you're determined not to put it back on!

Mrs. Williams: Do help yourself to more meat and potatoes.

You: ....

Mrs. W: On a diet! You could do with putting on a few extra pounds. I don't understand you young people...why do you all want to be so skinny these days? Have some more cabbage – that won't hurt you.

You: ....

Mrs. W: Aren't you? Well, I hope you've got room for a bit of pudding. I've made a lovely fresh cream trifle. You must try that.

You: ....

Mrs. W: Thank you very much, it's kind of you to say so. Now why don't you try this...it's English Cheddar and I don't suppose you've come across it before.

You: ....

Lewes–a county town

County town of East Sussex
80 kms from London
12 kms from Brighton
Pop. 14,250
Early Closing: Wed.
Winter min. temp. 2°C
Summer max. temp. 21°C

Norman Castle built at end of 11th century: 2 mounds, 2 towers.
Museum includes stocks and whipping post.
Famous Battle of Lewes in 1264.

Tourist Centre
187 High St. Tel.6151
Hospital Tel. 4153
Police Tel. 5432
Fire Tel. 3333

Hourly trains to London (Victoria) 55 mins.
B.R. Tel. 4618

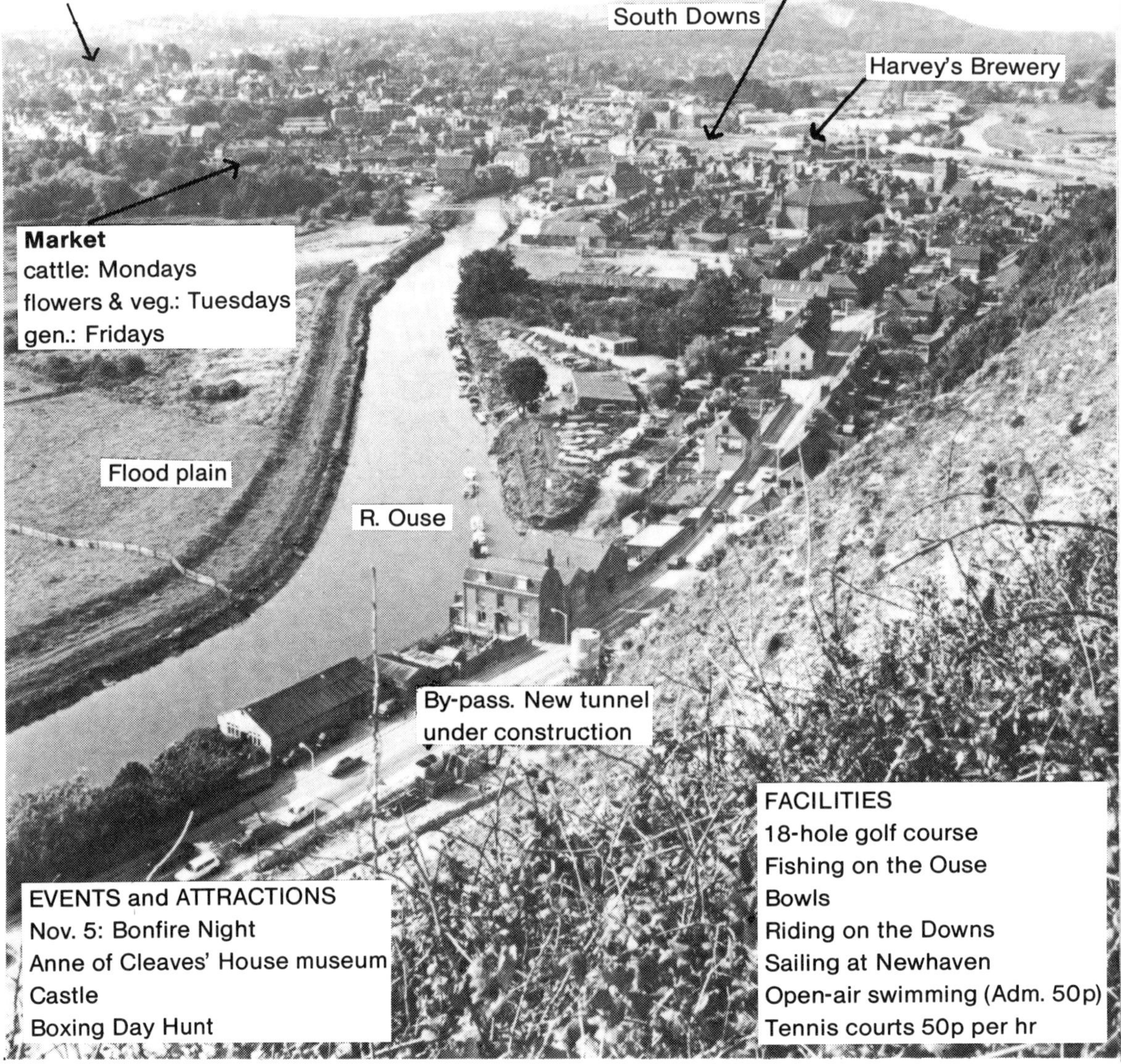

Phoning and posting

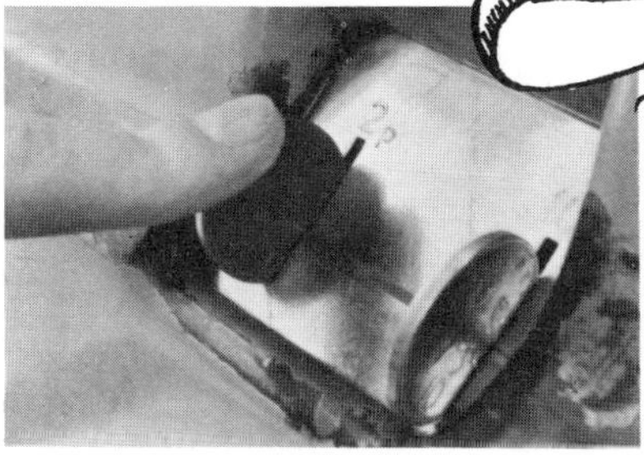

The phone

How would you say these numbers:

01 353 7891
0892 5311
0226 6444

If you want to ring these numbers from a call box in Piccadilly Circus, what exactly do you dial?

Complete this telephone conversation:

Michelle: Hello 4137

Brian: ....

M: Yes. Is that Brian? How are you? I haven't seen you for ages.

B: ....

M: Oh, I'm sorry to hear that. I didn't know. Are you better now?

B: ....

M: Well, I'm going away for the weekend but I'm not doing anything on Friday night.

B: ....

M: That'd be great. I'd love to.

B: ....

M: Could you make it a bit later – I don't usually get in until about 6.30.

B: ....

The post

Have you ever thought about what you can and can't send through the post? For example, the British Post Office doesn't allow red packets or envelopes or "any other colour likely to cause strain on the eyes of the Post Office staff. Cards, labels or envelopes should preferably be white. There is no objection to other colours (except red) provided that the shades are not glaring, vivid, dazzling in effect, or too dark". *(Post Office Guide)*

In the *Post Office Guide,* there is a long list of things that you can't send through the post to certain countries. You can't send books or photographs to Poland, Japanese shaving brushes to Uganda, communist literature to Peru, or old boots and shoes to South Africa.

Here are some other things which certain countries don't allow to be sent in by post. Look at the clues and see if you can match the thing to the country.

Bolivia China Switzerland Mexico Greece Sweden Russia Denmark Saudi Arabia

Watches Soap Playing cards Toothpaste Horoscopes Sugar Chewing-gum Pork Honey

Clues

A large and timeless country.
Paradise for Latin American dentists.
There's no future in cuckoo clocks.
They're sweet enough in Stockholm.
Forget poker – just enjoy the Ouzo.
Banned by religion.
Vodka is preferred to this Western habit here.
"To bee, or not to bee?" Not in Hamlet's country.
Wash well before you visit this high-up capital city.

Cheap travel connections

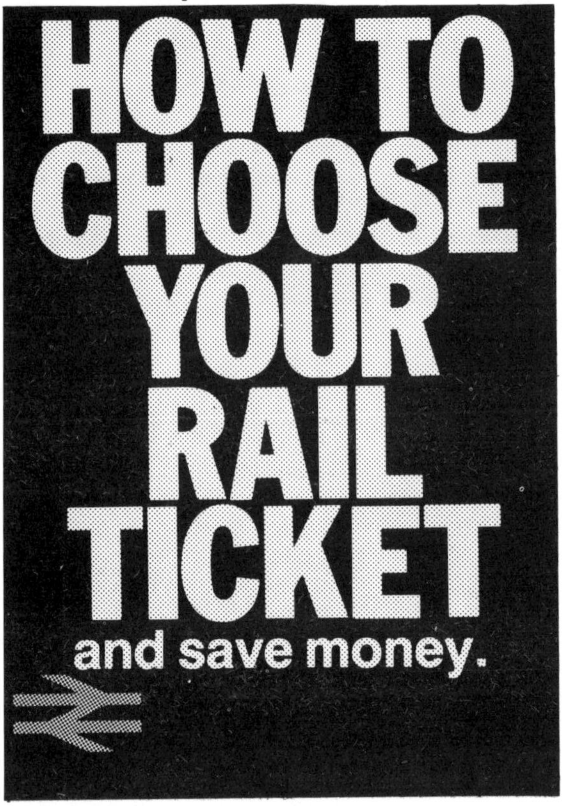

Here are some ways to save money when travelling by train.

Awayday Return

This ticket can save you up to 45 per cent on the standard fare. You have to travel after the rush-hour period in the morning, Mon - Fri, but can travel at any time on Sat, Sun or Bank Holidays.

Big City Savers

There are special low-priced tickets on certain trains. You have to book in advance – at the latest by 1600 the day before you travel. It's first come, first served and numbers are limited, so don't delay.

Fare Deal Bargains

These are for longer trips. In addition to Standard Tickets, which can be used on any train, there are different fare bargains to help you on special trips:

WEEKEND RETURNS are available for most journeys over 60 miles. Go on Fri, Sat or Sun, and return the same weekend on Sat, Sun or Mon, and save up to 35 per cent on the standard fare.

MONTHLY RETURNS are available for most journeys over 65 miles. Go any day and return within a month. Monthly returns save you up to 25 per cent on the standard fare.

Family Railcard

For £10 this railcard allows you to take a second adult and up to 4 children for only 50p each, when you buy single, return or Awayday return tickets. You can travel as often as you like until the card becomes out of date.

Which is the best ticket to buy if:

1. You're planning a day trip to visit an old friend. You don't mind which day of the week you go.

2. You want to go to Scotland for a week leaving London on a Friday.

3. You are married and have a child aged 12. The three of you want to visit your sister for the weekend. She lives at the seaside, about 80 miles away.

4. You have a business appointment at 10.00 a.m. in Manchester. The rail journey there will take you about two hours.

5. You live in London and you want to go to Bristol for a week. You don't mind when you travel.

IN THE NEWS

Local radio

Until some years ago the BBC was the only radio company allowed to broadcast in Britain. Today it no longer has this monopoly: 19 independent radio stations have been opened and there are plans for more.

Advertising pays their operating costs and they aim to provide a truly *local* community service. The BBC has also opened local radio stations.

Both services broadcast music programmes, quizzes, phone-ins, discussions about local events and regular news bulletins. Peak listening time is between 7 and 9 in the morning but late-night programmes are also popular. Most of the commercial stations broadcast round the clock. But why has local radio become so popular – especially with younger listeners? How is it different from national radio?

Here are some examples of ways in which local stations have helped their local communities:

In the hot dry summer of 1976 there was a serious fire in the North Yorkshire countryside. Radio Cleveland broadcast an appeal for volunteers to help the firemen and got 150 within half an hour.

After a mining disaster Piccadilly Radio sponsored a concert in Manchester. £7000 was raised and was given to the miners' families. Every day the station also gives details of credit cards that have been lost or stolen in the area. This service is very useful for local shopkeepers.

Radio Tees has a regular spot in which details of lost pets are given to listeners.

When several people in Middlesborough became ill with polio, Radio Tees provided information about vaccination centres.

In the farming area of Cumbria, Radio Carlisle broadcasts information about orphan lambs, or sheep whose lambs have died, so that farmers can contact each other.

Some areas have a high proportion of immigrants. BRMB radio in Birmingham has a weekly programme of music, news information and ads for Asian listeners broadcast in Hindustani.

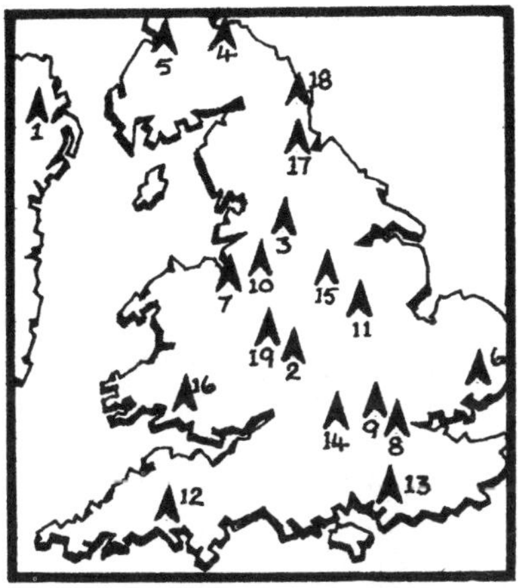

Independent radio companies

In Ipswich, there were serious floods in 1976 which caused huge power failures. Radio Orwell provided vital information on the air and helped prevent a major disaster.

What other help do you think a local radio station can give to an area?

One of the most popular and successful commercial stations is Capital Radio which began in 1973 and now has over 5 million regular listeners in the London area. Of Londoners in the 15-24 age-group, an incredible 4 out of 5 tune in to Capital every week. Here are some reasons why.

Its Jobfinder service invites young jobless people to drop into the office or phone 01-636 3261. They are given details of job opportunities and the service is free.

If you're looking for someone to share your flat, Nicky Horne's Tuesday evening programme takes details by phone and publishes a free list on Wednesday for people who are looking for accommodation.

If you've lost touch with old friends or relations, write to Michael Aspel and he'll read out your message in the "Where are you now?" part of his Tuesday morning programme.

Open Line on Wednesdays gives similar help on the air for people who phone in with emotional problems.

Swop Shop gives you the chance to exchange anything for anything by phoning on Thursday mornings around 10.00a.m.

1 Belfast
2 Birmingham
3 Bradford
4 Edinburgh
5 Glasgow
6 Ipswich
7 Liverpool
8 London
9 London
10 Manchester
11 Nottingham
12 Plymouth
13 Portsmouth
14 Reading
15 Sheffield and Rotherham
16 Swansea
17 Teesside
18 Tyne/Wear
19 Wolverhampton /Black Country

SNAPSHOT SESSION

A day out

In the same way that New York and Paris don't represent life in America and France, so London doesn't truly reflect life in Britain. A country town is more typical of our way of life.

Imagine you are spending a day with a friend in such a place. These photos are a selection of some of the signs you might see.

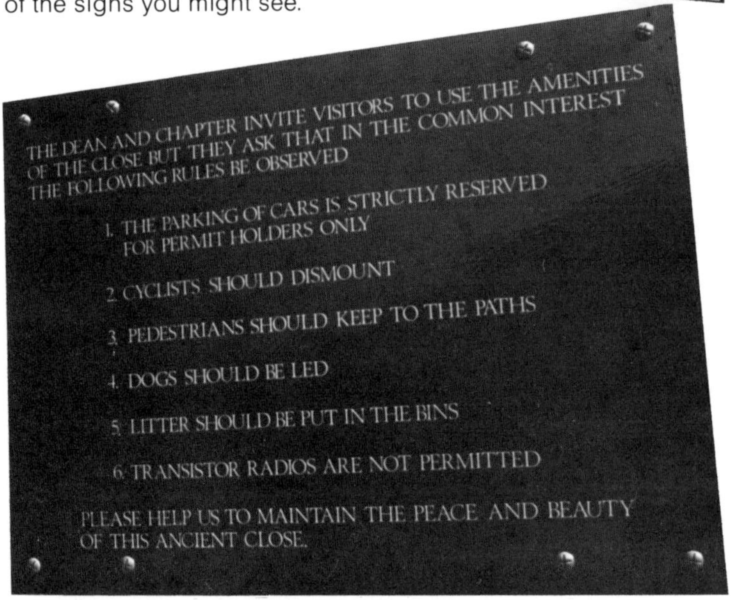

1. When you arrive, you head for the Cathedral; in the grounds, there's a sign:

a) What do you need if you want to park your car here?
b) Are bicycles allowed here?
c) What must dogs wear?

2. After seeing the Cathedral, you go to the town centre. On the way you see a message on a tree.

a) Would the owner give you anything if you found this cat?
b) What's the cat wearing?

3. You see this notice in a shop window. What's it about?

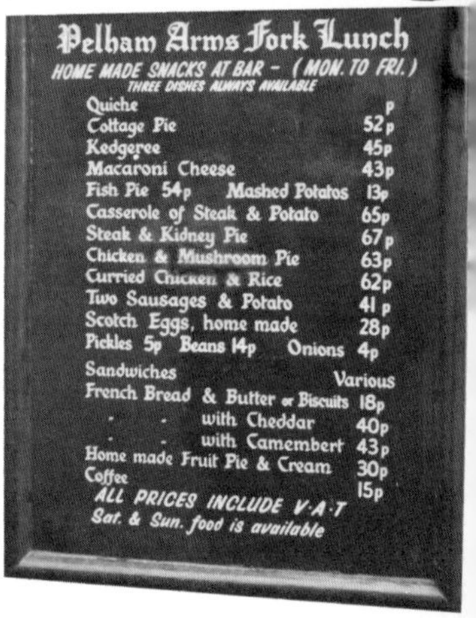

4. You both feel peckish so you decide to have an early lunch. This pub menu catches your eye.

a) What do you think a Fork Lunch is?
b) What kind of food could you order on a Saturday?
c) If you had Chicken and Mushroom Pie with Beans, followed by French Bread and Cheddar and a cup of coffee, how much would your bill be?

5. After lunch, you stroll down to the Castle.

a) How much do you have to pay?
b) Where do you buy the tickets?
c) Two reductions are offered. What are they?

> Have you noticed anything odd about this page? *E.g., where* did you spend your day?

An interview with a landlord

PUB seems a funny word. Why are pubs called pubs?

Yes, it is an odd word but really it's just short for 'public house', a place that has a special licence to sell drinks to people.

Why do most pubs have signs hanging outside them?

Because up to the beginning of this century, most people couldn't read, so a picture was the easiest way to show travellers where they could get a drink.

Ah, I see, but one thing I've noticed in Britain is that a lot of the pubs have the same name. I've seen at least three called The Red Lion. Why is this?

Well, many years ago, huge areas of Britain were owned by a small number of families, and clever innkeepers named their pubs after these families who each had their own family symbol. For example, a Red Lion was the Gaunt family's symbol. The Tudors had a greyhound, that's why so many pubs all over the country have the same name.

Other pubs got their names from religious events, ways of travelling, sports, jobs, famous people, famous battles and so on...so you see – studying pub names is a really good way of learning a bit about our history.

I noticed when I came in that your pub's called a "free house". What does that mean?

Unfortunately it doesn't mean that the drinks are free! It's just that

most pubs are owned by big breweries like Watneys or Charringtons and so they only sell their own beer. But some landlords, like me, are lucky enough to own their own pubs and so they're free to sell any beer they like from any brewery.

Really....well this beer is lovely, it's very different from lager.

Yes, it's what we call real ale.

What's that?

Ah, that's a good question – and one that confuses a lot of tourists. Real ale's usually made by small local breweries so each type has a different taste. It's normally much stronger than the beer made by big breweries – when you're travelling round England you should try to taste some of the different types.

I will, I didn't realise there was so much choice. Do you have food here, I'm getting a bit hungry?

Yes, we've got sandwiches, pies, and a "Ploughman's" – do you know what that is?

I've no idea! What is it?

Well, it's bread, butter, cheese and pickled onions. Farmworkers used to have it for their lunch when they were working in the fields. Why don't you try one?

Mm — I will....

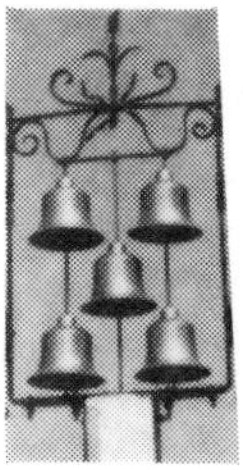

What are the names of these pubs?

ANIMALS IN BRITAIN

Working animals

Richard commutes from Tunbridge Wells to Charing Cross every day. This difficult journey is made easier with the help of Raffles, his guide dog. Lorraine met him on the train....

Lorraine : What a lovely dog – how long have you had her?

Richard : ...Um...since July 1978.

L : Isn't it a bit unusual to have an alsation as a guide dog, aren't they usually labradors?

R : Yes, you're right. I did have a labrador before Raffles, but we were walking through London one day when an IRA bomb went off and it frightened her so much that she became unreliable.

L : Oh, I'm sorry to hear that. What happened to her?

R : She's fine, she's leading a life of luxury with a family in Rye.

L : What about Raffles, though, could you commute without her for instance?

R : Mm, yes...but much more slowly. On the other hand, people often overestimate what guide dogs can do.

L : Really – in what way?

R : Well, it's impossible to train them to cope with modern traffic, especially in London. The best she can do is to warn me of a dangerous situation.

L : How can she do that?

R : Simply by sitting down and refusing to move. I have to stand still and just hope that the driver misses me.

L : That must be a horrific experience....

R : Yes, it's not much fun!

L : Can I ask how much you paid for Raffles'

R : 50p.

L : What?

R : 50p...any blind person can buy a dog fo 50p. Of course a lot of people pa more voluntarily, but the minimun price is 50p.

L : So public contributions, on flag days fo example, are really important...

R : Absolutely. The money, as you can see, i put to good use: these dogs have a ver valuable working life.

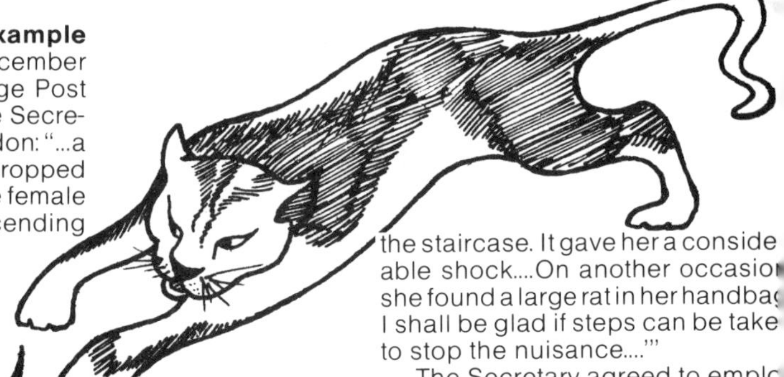

Here's a more unusual example of working animals. In December 1920 the Manager of a large Post Office in Bristol wrote to the Secretary of the Post Office in London: "...a night or two ago, a large rat dropped on the shoulder of one of the female cleaners as she was descending the staircase. It gave her a conside able shock....On another occasio she found a large rat in her handba I shall be glad if steps can be take to stop the nuisance....'"

The Secretary agreed to emplo a cat at the wage of one shilling week. Cats are still employed toda in some Post Offices in order to kee Britain's mail moving.

Tourist centres

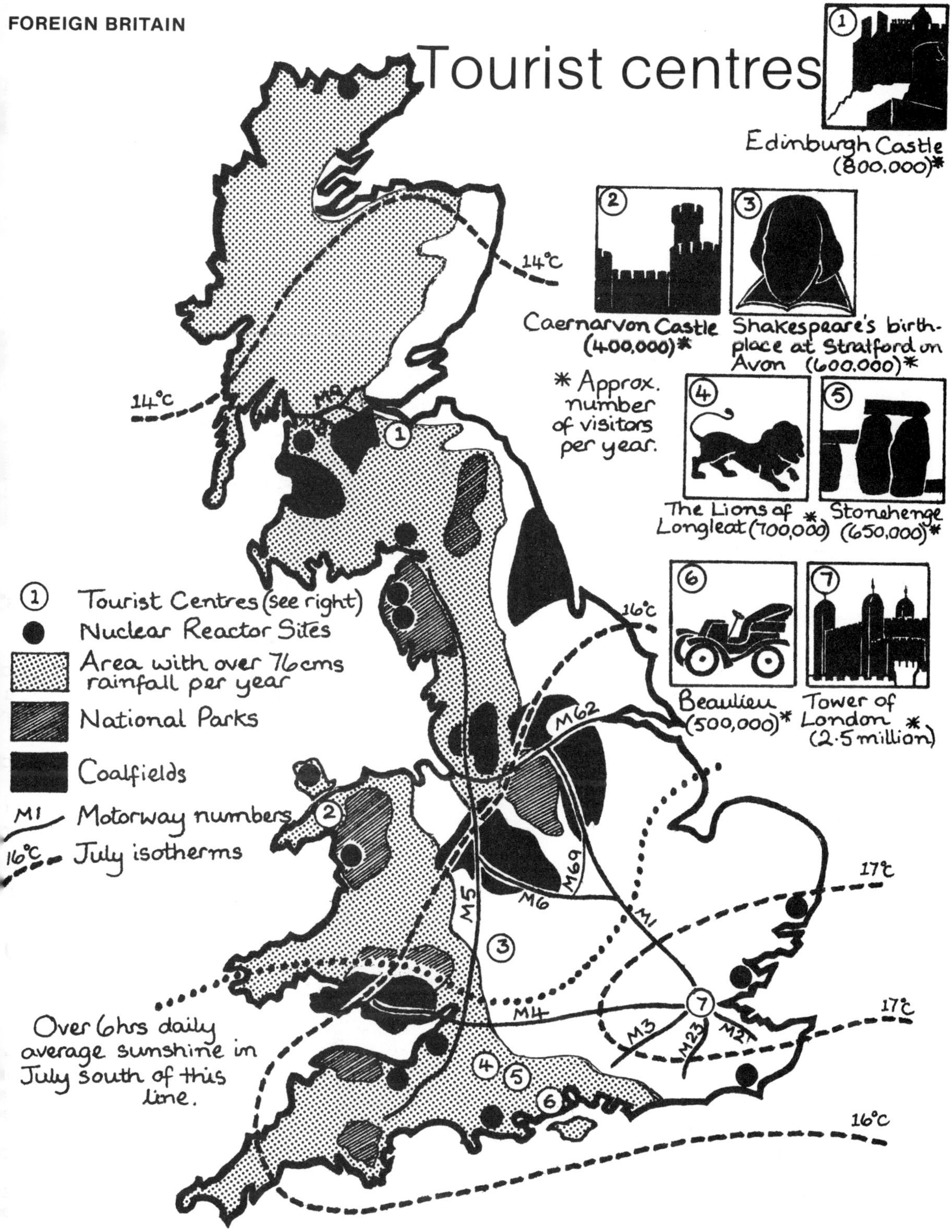

Spot the Difference

Can you find 10 differences between the first drawing and the second?

Tongue-twisters

How many times can you say these without making a mistake?

She sells sea-shells by the sea-shore;
the shells that she sells are sea-shells, I'm sure.

Round and round the rugged rocks the ragged rascal ran.

Peter Piper picked a peck of pickled pepper,
a peck of pickled pepper Peter Piper picked.
If Peter Piper picked a peck of pickled pepper,
where's the peck of pickled pepper
Peter Piper picked?

The Leith Police dismisseth us.

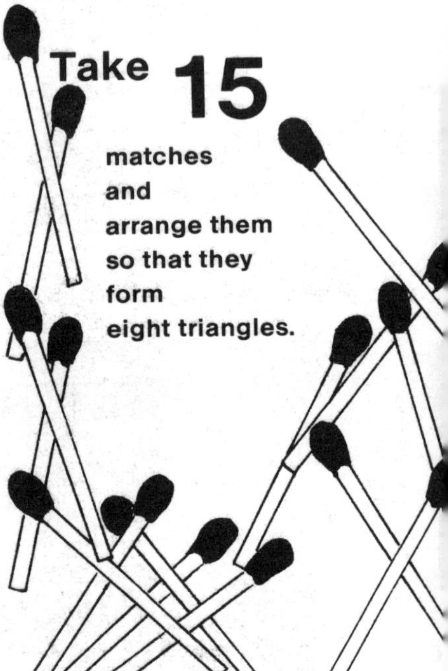

Take 15 matches and arrange them so that they form eight triangles.

The Irish joke

People often tell jokes about other nationalities. In Britain there are thousands of jokes about the Irish. Here are some of them. What do they tell you about the Irish – from the British point of view? Do you have any jokes about the British?

There was an Irish pilot who was coming in to land at Heathrow Airport. The control tower asked for his "height and position". The pilot replied, "1 m 50 and sitting in the front."

What is written at the bottom of an Irish milk bottle?

What is there at the top of an Irish ladder?

There was an Irishman working on a building site, who had an accident. His ear was cut off by a piece of machinery, so he went to see his boss and told him what had happened. His boss said that they should go and look for the ear because the doctors might be able to put it back on. After a few minutes the boss shouted, "Look, here it is!" The Irishman looked at it and said, "No, that isn't mine – mine had a pencil behind it."

"Why are Irish jokes so stupid?"

"Because otherwise the English wouldn't understand them!"

Can you fill in the blank spaces?

Leslie is not Bob's brother, but Bob is Leslie's brother. What relation is Leslie to Bob?

Can you arrange the words of this joke to fit the picture?

clocks...do...two... times...why... different...show... those...?

because...one...need... same...the...we'd... time...if...showed... they...only...!

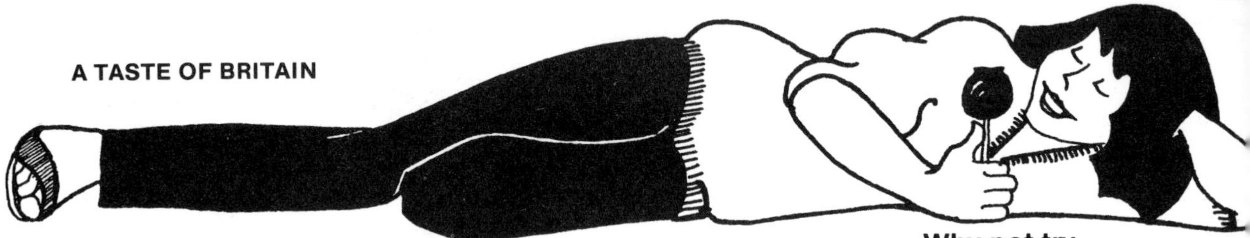

Descriptions and opinions

sour "off" soggy gooey creamy sickly mushy stringy rich sticky sharp crunchy bitter chewy

Can you use these words to describe the foods below?

a lemon last week's milk a cucumber peanuts undercooked cake toffees a bar of milk chocolate too many bars of milk chocolate! old green beans very strong coffee cream-filled meringues overcooked boiled potatoes

Students' opinions about English food

"English people don't cook with love...."

"You can't make coffee in England, it tastes of nothing and it's sour."

"I don't like English breakfasts because I don't like hot food in the morning."

"English people eat only for living, not for enjoying"

"I think English food is quite nice. I'm surprised because all my friends say that it's awful."

What's your opinion?

Why not try making these crunchy toffee apples?

Toffee apples don't keep well and you should eat them on the same day as you make them. You will need:

6 ice cream sticks, 6 crisp eating apples (*Granny Smiths are best),* 150gms of sugar, 75ml water, 1 teaspoon lemon juice, a heavy saucepan and a large piece of foil rubbed with a little oil.

What to do. We've mixed up these instructions. Can you put them in the right order?

Then turn up the heat and boil the mixture for a couple of minutes.

Pull out the stems and push the sticks into them.

If the toffee in the pan gets too thick, turn on the heat for a short time.

Wash and dry the apples.

Wait for the sugar to dissolve – don't stir.

Stand each apple on its end on the foil.

When it becomes a golden colour, turn off the heat.

Put the sugar, lemon and water into the saucepan over a LOW heat.

Quickly dip each apple into the toffee, one at a time.

Put in a cool place and leave them for a couple of hours – if you can!

Hold the apple over the pan until the toffee gets hard.

What is happening here?

The National Centre for Alternative Technology

The people at Britain's National Centre of Alternative Technology in Wales are trying to find ways of using less energy. They also believe that we should make more use of natural resources like the sun, wind and water.

They grow their own food without using chemicals and keep animals to provide milk, meat and manure. The centre began in 1974 and about 80,000 people visit it every year.

Some people think that nuclear power is the answer to our energy problems. Others, including those at the NCAT believe that we must learn to use less energy and develop safer alternatives to nuclear power. Research into alternative technology is growing as the energy crisis gets worse.

Can you make sentences using these ideas and then think of more advantages and disadvantages?

Piccadilly Circus

Where did this odd name come from? No-one really knows. One idea is that in the late sixteenth century, a man called Robert Baker used to make shirt "frills" in this area. These were called "pickadills". The local people nicknamed his house "Pickadilly Hall" and eventually the area became known as Piccadilly.

But why is it called a circus? Because the buildings around it used to be curved in the shape of a circle.

What's the name of the statue? That's Eros.
When and why was it built? It was built in 1893 to honour Lord Shaftesbury who helped the local poor people. It represented his love and kindness.

At first, people were shocked because the statue had no clothes. This was no way to honour a Lord! Especially in 1893! It was soon nicknamed Eros, the Greek god of love – and the name has stayed ever since.

Trafalgar Square

Trafalgar Square was also built to honour a famous man – Admiral Nelson, who defeated the Spanish and French navies at Trafalgar in 1805. The 52m high column was built between 1839 and 1842.

At first, people disliked the 5m high statue of Nelson because it didn't really look like him. This was no way to honour an Admiral! Especially in 1840. They forgot that only the pigeons would be able to see his face.

There are two interesting things in the square that tourists often miss. The first is this police station in the south-east corner (one of the smallest in the world). The other is the standard measurement along the north wall of the square. These show the old British measurements.

There used to be a market in the square where people sold cloth. Marks were put on the wall so that they could measure the cloth against them. The Government decided to put the standard measurements into the wall so no-one could argue about the length of a foot or a yard.

Why do you think it was necessary to put the metal into the wall at 62°F (17°C)?

Two timetables

Dan Davies, aged 16.

	MON	TUES	WED	THURS	FRI	SAT
7.45-8.15	BREAKFAST					
8.45-8.55		CHURCH		CHURCH		
9.00-9.40		MATHS	MATHS	PHYSICS	BIOLOGY	MATHS
9.45-10.25		FRENCH	LATIN	FRENCH		ENGLIS
10.30-11.10	FRENCH	CHEMISTRY	ENGLISH	GEOGRAPHY	DIVINITY	
	MORNING BREAK					
11.40-12.20	GEOGRAPHY	GYM	FRENCH	ENGLISH	HISTORY	GEOGRAP
12.25-1.05	BIOLOGY		HISTORY	DIVINITY	LATIN	LATIN
1.15-1.45	LUNCH					
2.10-2.50	LATIN		CHEMISTRY		MATHS	
2.55-3.35	DIVINITY					
6.15-6.50	TEA					
PREP	FRENCH	FRENCH	GEOGRAPHY	LATIN	LATIN	GEOGRAP
	CHEMISTRY	MATHS	PHYSICS	BIOLOGY	MATHS	BIOLOG
	ENGLISH	CHEMISTRY	ENGLISH	PHYSICS	HISTORY	

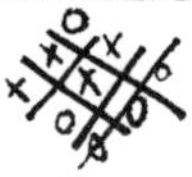

	MON	TUES	WED	THURS	FRI
8.55-9.20	TUTOR PERIOD				
9.20-9.50 / 9.50-10.20 / 10.20-10.50	Liberal Studies	French	P.E / R.E.	Pottery	Geography
	MORNING BREAK				
11.10-11.40 / 11.40-12.10 / 12.10-12.40	Integrated Science	Maths	Liberal Studies	Visual Studies	Mass Media Studies
	DINNER				
13.40-14.10 / 14.10-14.40	Mass Media Studies	Liberal Studies	Maths	French	Integrated Science
14.40-15.10 / 15.10-15.40	Pottery	Visual Studies	Geography	Liberal Studies	P.E
1½ hrs. At home	Lib. Studs. Int. Sc.	French Maths	Maths Geog.	Vis. Studies French	Geog. Mass Media Int. Sc.

Paul Bradb aged

LOOKING AHEAD

Reading palms

Kathy McKay has worked on Hastings pier for 14 years. She prefers reading palms because she thinks that they give a more accurate reading of the future than Tarot cards or crystal balls. When she started, most of her clients were women – today, just as many are men.

She always looks at both palms because the left one shows your real character while the right one shows the character you would like people to think you have!

Here are some of the things she told us about reading palms:

When the Finger of Jupiter is very long, it means you are big-headed and bossy.

A square, fat Finger of Saturn shows a serious-minded person. A pointed one shows a more light-hearted kind of person.

People who have a long Finger of Sun, one that's almost as long as the Finger of Jupiter are creative and artistic – they are the ones who want to "get to the top".

When the Finger of Mercury is long and well-shaped, it shows a born leader.

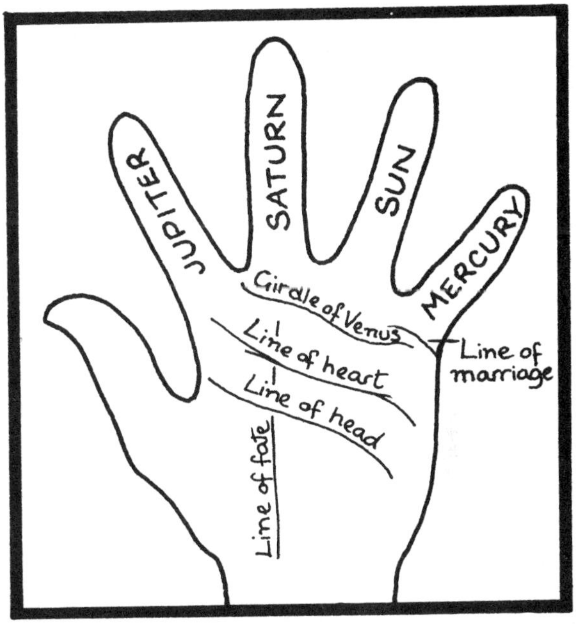

The lines on the palm are very important:

When the Line of Fate is clearly marked, it shows that you're going to be "well-off". What do you think it means if it isn't marked clearly?

A strong Line of Heart indicates that you are warm-hearted. A weak line shows that you are tight-fisted.

A strong Line of Head shows that you're brainy. What do you think a weak line shows?

Nervous people have a strong girdle of Venus.

Look at the length of the line of marriage. *A long line shows a long and happy marriage.* What about a broken line?

Look what Kathy McKay wrote about this person. What's going to happen to her?

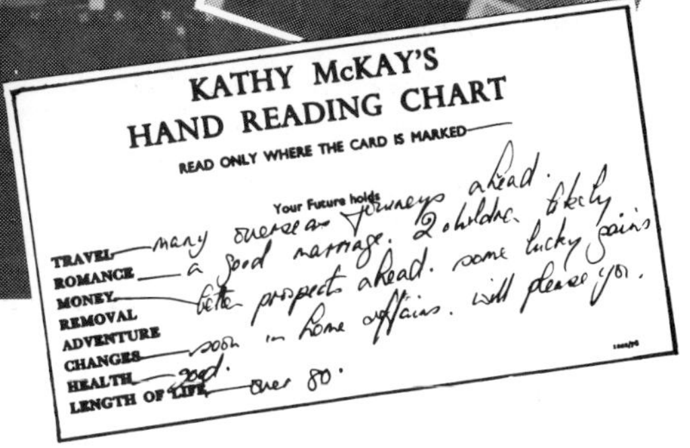
KATHY McKAY'S
HAND READING CHART
READ ONLY WHERE THE CARD IS MARKED

Your Future holds

TRAVEL — many overseas journeys ahead.
ROMANCE — a good marriage. 2 children likely
MONEY — better prospects ahead. some lucky gains
REMOVAL
ADVENTURE
CHANGES — soon in home affairs. will please you.
HEALTH — good.
LENGTH OF LIFE — over 80.

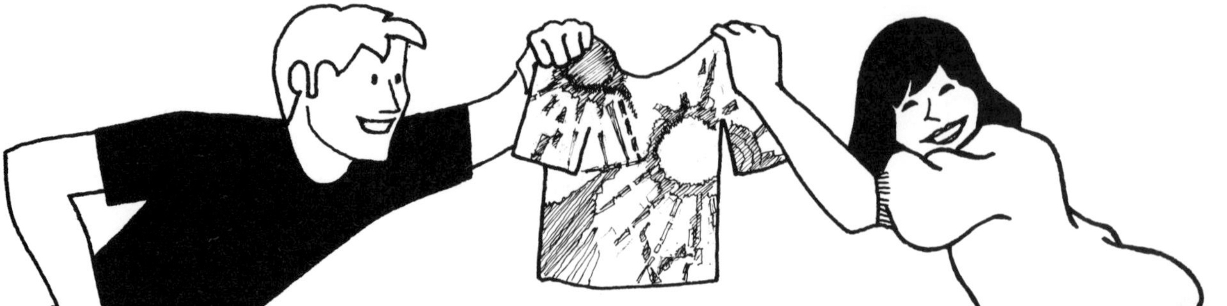

MAKE AND TAKE HOME

Tie-dyeing

Tie-and-dye is a cheap and easy way of changing a plain T-shirt into something special. Every T-shirt you do will be different. It's exciting, too, because you can never be sure exactly how the shirt will look when you've finished!

All you need is a cotton T-shirt, some cold-water dye (large department stores always have it), a spoon and some string.

First, roll up your T-shirt tightly. Tie the string round it in different places and in different directions as tightly as you can. This is very important because it stops the dye from colouring the whole of the T-shirt. You can make even more interesting patterns if you tie dried peas or small stones into the material with the string.

Mix the dye with water. The instructions on the tin will tell you how much to use. Then put the T-shirt into the dye. Read the instructions again to see how long to leave it there.

When it's ready, wash the T-shirt in clean water, untie the string and let it dry.

You can add another colour to your T-shirt by tying it in different places and repeating the dyeing with another colour.

Potato Prints

Tie and dye is fun because you get a surprise at the end, but you might prefer to have more control over the way you dye your clothes. Potato prints are also easy to do, but if you are careful, you can get very neat results.

Slice a potato in half, then cut out a design on it *(see diagram)*. Then fill your T-shirt completely with crumpled newspaper to stop the dye from going on to the parts you don't want dyed. Dip the potato into the dye and press it carefully on to the T-shirt.

Leave it to dry completely, then put it into a mixture of cold water and salt. This fixes the dye and stops it from colouring the rest of the T-shirt when you wash it.

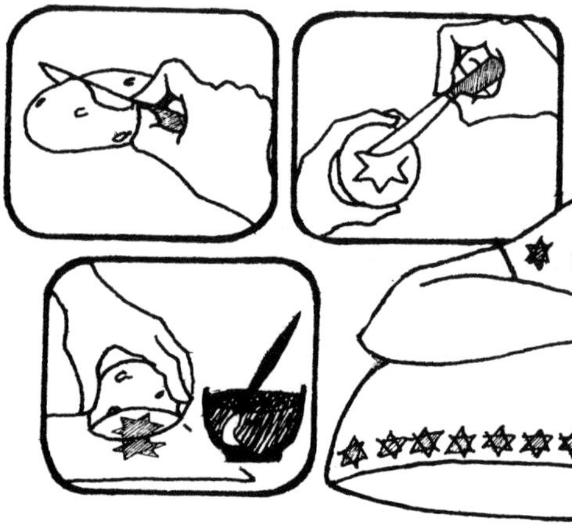

Advanced section

Words at work

English spelling often confuses foreigners – and the British! Can you spot the spelling mistakes in these photos?

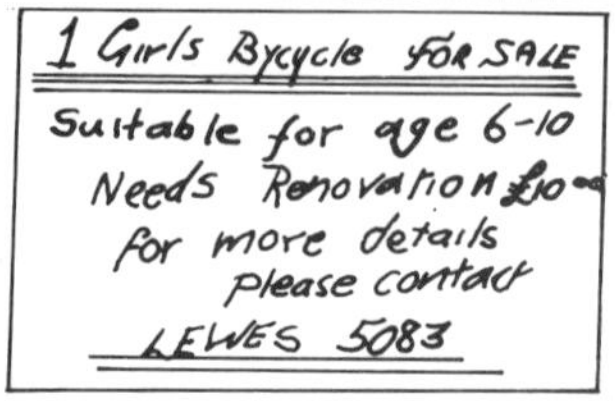

Here's part of a sign – can you complete it?

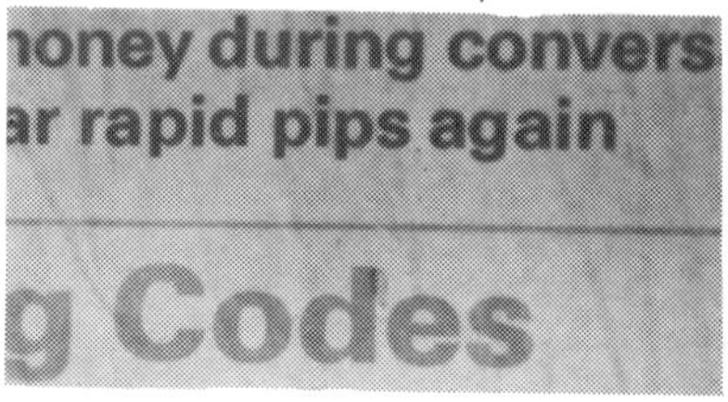

See if you can complete these words by reading their definitions:

C..L.P..NE
a transparent wrapping material

C.B...T
a kind of entertainment

H..I.O..E.
a kind of aircraft

I..L....B..
easy to burn

O...C..N
a maker of spectacles

Now why not have a go at writing your own? Try them out on another student.

Can you find two meanings in each of these advertisements?

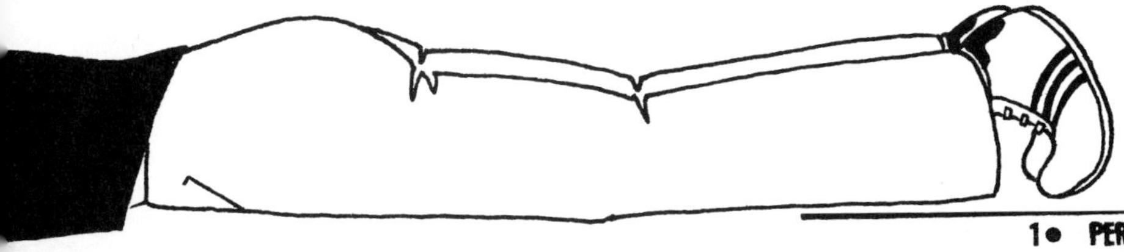

Family life
3 ways of looking at it

EXPENDITURE of income

(percentages)

19·1	Food
14.8	Housing
9·2	Car and running costs
8.1	Clothing
8	Alcohol
4.8	Fuel
4·6	Other durable goods
4.4	Meals out
4.2	Tobacco
3·3	Other travel
9.8	Other services
9·7	Other goods

1• PERSONAL

DAVID SHOULD BE IN A HOME, NOT A HOME

David is a 3½-year-old, with sandy hair and blue eyes and we think that if you saw him you would agree that he should not be living in a Residential Nursery where he has been for the last 2 years. He should be growing up in a family. He seems a bright child, unusually imaginative and he loves being read to and playing make-believe games. He sometimes retreats into himself and sucks his thumb and at other times he is boisterous and rather restless. He is confused and angry that he is not living with his mother. Because of his mother's difficulties she will not be visiting David in the foster home, but his social worker will take him occasionally to see her. We expect David to remain in the foster home for the rest of his childhood, but as he may take some time to settle we are prepared to pay an enhanced boarding out rate of up to £40 per week. David should be the youngest child by at least 3 years because he needs a lot of individual attention.

If you would like to find out more about David and live in London or the Home Counties, contact ... Team ... ster ... 4.

"...sometimes I dream about being an orphan. I could do anything I wanted, I wouldn't have to worry about hurting my parents...."

"The family is just another way for the State to control the people – only it's more subtle. Instead of using direct force to make people conform – it uses emotional blackmail...."

"...I love my family a lot, I just wish they'd learn to accept me as an adult equal and stop trying to interfere in my life all the time...."

"I hate visiting my family – it's all so false. There you are, stuck in a room with people you don't even like – but you're supposed to love them. I prefer my friends; I chose them myself...."

"My hairstyle, my clothes, my books, my boyfriend. Why do my parents control all this...?"

"Family life is based on exploitation. I exploit my parents for food, clothing and pocket-money – they exploit me by expecting me to be what they want in return for food, clothing and pocket-money. It's a vicious circle...."

Exploiting tourists

What to wear

sunglasses
comfortable shoes
casual jacket with large pockets

Where to go

seaside promenades
tourist traps
the London Underground
airports
banks and *bureaux de change*

Who to look for

people with two or more cameras
tans
souvenir T-shirts/shorts
bulging wallets
dictionaries/phrase-books

How to steal

A crude and dangerous method is to use a sharp knife to cut or slit handbags. It's more subtle to pick pockets. All you need is lots of practice!

What to sell

Be guided by the weather. **If it's hot,** sell ice-creams and chilled drinks. **If it's wet,** sell umbrellas. **If it's cold,** sell hot dogs.
Always add 50 per cent to the advertised price – tourists don't usually notice. If you're given five pounds, always give change for one. It often works! Do the same with 50p pieces. Talk quickly.

Some other methods:

GETTING THROUGH

Phone or post?

0---------4---4---4---4---8-------3--2-
0----------5----CLONK........BRRR-BRRR.....
BRRR-BRRR.... BRRR-BRRR........CLICK."Hoozat?.....
Sorry, is that you Mum?........ Airdrie 420?....Where?....
.... Scotland!.... Sorry, wrong number. I'd better get off the line
quick..........................I said.......Oh, never mind, bye."....CLICK.
BRRRRRRR.0---------4---4---4---
8-------

Wouldn't a letter say it better? *Basildon Bond*
by John Dickinson

"Hello Mary?...It's me...Roger. ...You know, Roger....How are you?...Long time...I'm well ...Been a few weeks, hasn't it? ...Listen, I'm sorry about that party...Don't you remember? That party...Oh never mind... And see you soon too...Maybe one day....Yes, who knows? ...Goodbye...Goodbye Mary ...Goodbye."

Wouldn't a letter say it better?
Basildon Bond
by John Dickinson

"Hello Joyce?...Who's that? ...Oh, Peter. Hello Peter. Could you fetch your mummy please? ...It's your auntie Carol. How do you know it's your auntie Carol? Because I said so, Peter.....Now could you fetch?....Yes I'd love to hear your nursery rhyme, Peter ....And you want me to hear your alphabet too?............. ....Well done, Peter......Now could you fetch? ...And your two-times table, as well?"

Wouldn't a letter say it better?
Basildon Bond
by John Dickinson

A Londoner's map of Britain

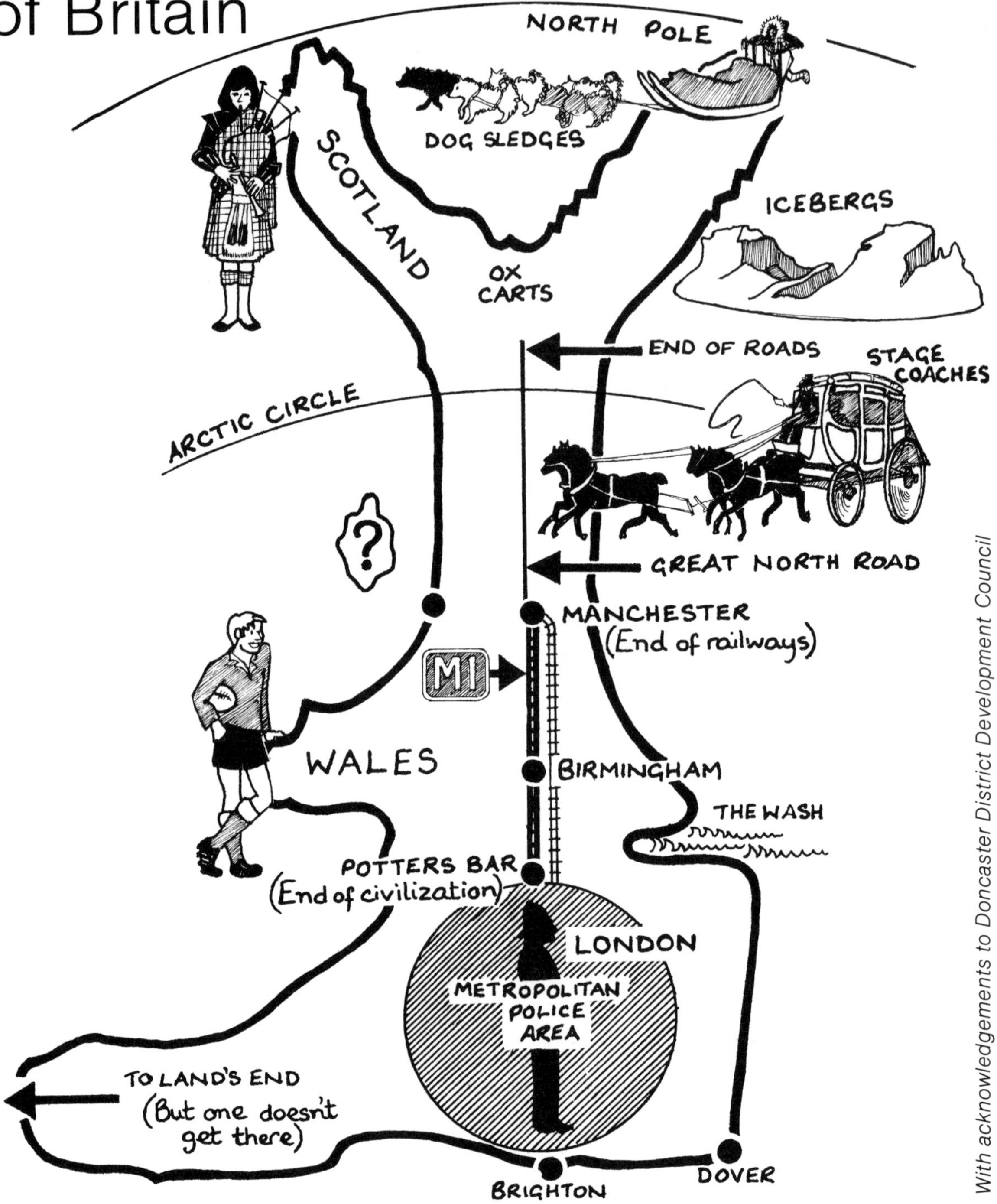

With acknowledgements to Doncaster District Development Council

IN THE NEWS

The British Press

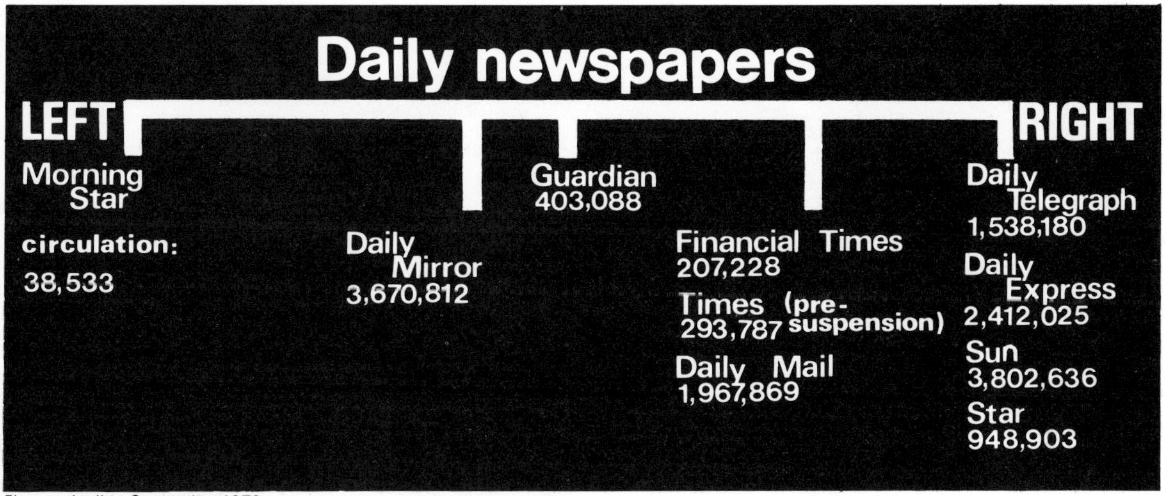

Figures April to September 1979

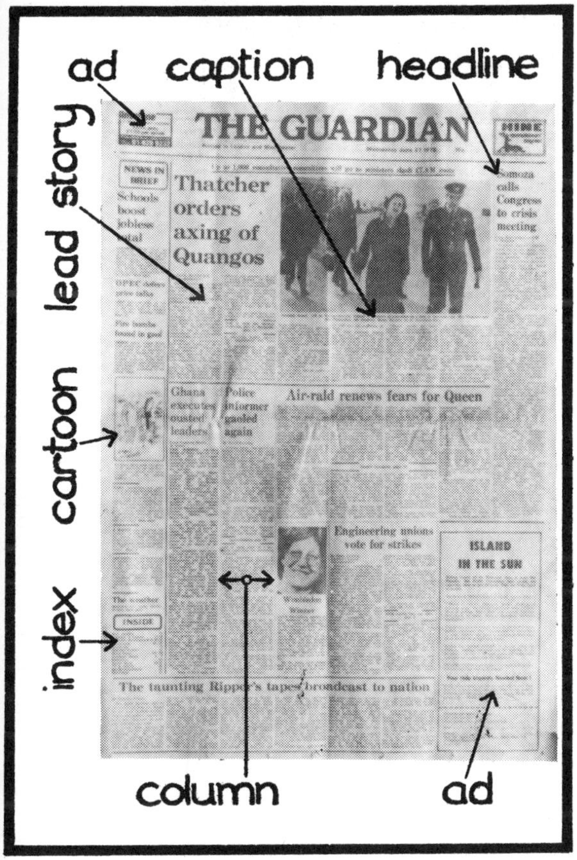

What would you expect to find inside these sections of a newspaper?

Financial Overseas Classifieds
Home Arts Diary Stars

Newspaper headlines use English in a special way. They are usually short and dramatic. Look at these headlines and work out how they have been shortened:

Man bites dog

DC 10 in bomb blast

Cloud over oil talks

Ex model weds MP

Queen to visit China

Mr C jets to summit

Princess quizzed in nude-killer hunt

Look out for:

Shortened words
Missing words
Use of tenses
Word changes
Exaggeration
Dramatic usage

A night out

Brighton, as you probably know, is a famous holiday town on the south coast of England. Young visitors like it because there's lots of night-life and easily available information.

Look at the round picture. This guide can be bought in most local newsagents. What would you ask for?

If you couldn't get a copy of the guide, what else could you buy to find out about evening entertainments?

△ Perhaps you'll decide to do something a little more cultural – like these people.

Where are they and what are they doing?

For fans of black soul music, Dennis Brown is a must. If you decide to go and see him on the spur of the moment, how much will it cost you? ▽

△
Brighton has many different kinds of entertainment.

What sport would you be interested in if you decided to go here, and how much would it cost?

What would be the best time to arrive?

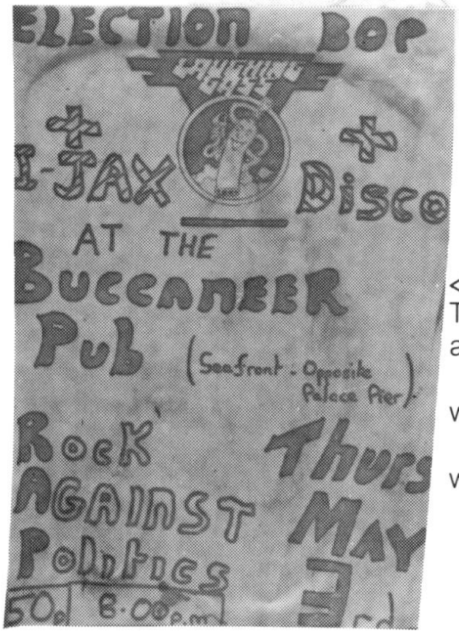

◁
The Buccaneer has other attractions for those who aren't keen on sport.

You'd probably be interested in two things if you went here. What would they be?

Your friend wants to come too, but doesn't know where it is. Can you tell her?

Is there any live music at the "Bop"?

A short history

Most foreigners find British pubs both fascinating and frustrating. Fascinating because they are unique to Great Britain and not at all like the bars you find in most other countries; and frustrating because of their peculiar opening and closing hours. In fact, much of the long history of pubs in Britain is to do with people who wanted to drink and others who wanted to stop them.

The development of pubs and the laws surrounding them is an interesting way of learning a little about our social history. Foreigners often think of tea as the British national drink, but compared to beer-drinking, tea-drinking is a very recent development.

Beer has been drunk in Britain since before the Roman invasion. The earliest breweries were part of

monasteries and as early as 695 AD the King of Kent was making laws in an attempt to stop priests from getting drunk.

The monasteries also provided food and beds for travellers. During the Middle Ages, it became so popular to make pilgrimages to famous religious shrines that inns had to be built because the monasteries could not look after the increasing numbers of pilgrims.

By the late 16th Century, drunkenness was a real problem and laws were passed to restrict drinking-hours. In 1606, a law was passed which stated that the purpose of inns was to lodge "wayfaring people only". Travellers were allowed to buy drinks at times forbidden to local people. However, the ingenuity of the dedicated drinkers got round this problem and the result was that the locals would simply move on to the next town or village when they wanted to continue drinking after "time" in their own village!

In the 19th Century, cheap gin appeared in Britain. It was very popular among poor people. Drunkenness again increased and more laws were passed. The Temperance Society was formed to fight against "the demon drink". This group of dedicated teetotallers tried to persuade people to abstain from drinking by getting them to "sign the pledge". Today's equivalent of the Temperance Society is Alcoholics Anonymous, which brings alcoholics together at weekly meetings and gives them a chance to help and support one another.

In spite of the various attempts to curb drinking, or stamp it out completely, pubs continue to provide a major part of British social

life. Their opening and closing-hours are still restricted by law although there have been recommendations recently for big changes, including extending licensing hours and admitting children.

But nothing has happened yet. It may be that having lived with our strange laws for so long, we've decided that we don't really mind them after all, and that tourists will just have to learn to put up with them too!

Put Animals into Politics!

All governments have allowed cruelty to animals.

Now is the time to stop it!

A large number of animal welfare and protection societies have come together in a single movement for the purpose of putting animals into politics. This unity is unique. We have six areas of immediate concern and we know that many thousands of people are looking to Parliament to introduce measures for the protection and welfare of animals in this country. OUR SIX AREAS OF CONCERN ARE: (Not in order of priority).

1 FACTORY FARMING

Where battery hens, calves and pigs are imprisoned in small cages, often for LIFE.

2 EXPERIMENTS ON LIVING ANIMALS

Where living animals are used for some highly questionable experiments and for testing cosmetics and other non-medical products which frequently cause acute pain and suffering.

3 TREATMENT OF HORSES

Where horses are treated cruelly by exposure and neglect. Where horses are transported hundreds of miles for slaughter to provide meat for the Continental table.

4 EXPORT OF LIVE FARM ANIMALS

Where farm animals suffer hardship and cruelty during transport both for overseas slaughter and further fattening.

5 DOGS IN THE COMMUNITY

Where dogs are left to stray, unwanted, and where the majority remain unlicensed, without a properly regulated system of centralised or local control.

6 BLOOD SPORTS

Where Public Opinion Polls indicate that the majority of people are in favour of banning "blood sports." That is, the hunting with hounds of otters, stags, hares and foxes and also live hare coursing.

The protection of animals against wanton and avoidable cruelty is of serious public concern. There can be no doubt of the importance of this subject. NOW is the time for POSITIVE ACTION. More and more voters are waiting to know where the political parties stand on this moral issue. Ask YOUR M.P. or Parliamentary candidates.

10 Queensferry Street, Edinburgh EH2 4PG. Telephone 031-225 2116

Chairman: Lord Houghton of Sowerby CH

General Election Co-ordinating Committee for Animal Protection

Put animals into politics

1. What is the main concern of the *Put Animals into Politics* campaign?

2. Can you explain the words "stray" and "wanton"?

3. What meat comes from a calf imprisoned in a cage for its short life?

4. What makes this campaign unique?

5. What do most British people think about hunting?

We don't eat horsemeat in Britain and no-one seems to know the reason for this. Any ideas?

Does this page confirm or change any opinions you had about the British and animals?

Ethnic minorities

Ethnic minorities often provoke emotional and uninformed opinions. In Britain there is a Commission for Racial Equality which tries to inform public opinion of the true facts rather than the myths. For example, many British people think that Pakistanis are the largest immigrant group but the bar-graph *(right)* shows that this is untrue. What **does** it show?

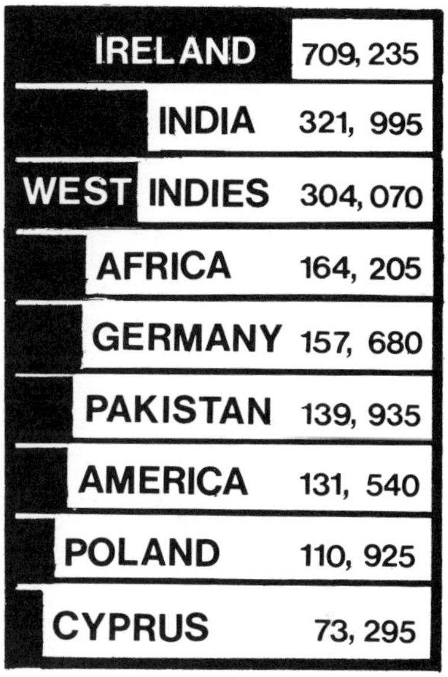

Here are some other myths that some people believe – and the facts.

MYTH: Immigration is making Britain an overcrowded island.
FACT: Since 1964 more people have left the UK each year than have entered. In 1976, 170,000 people came to live in Britain and 210,000 left, a net loss of 40,000. *(Office of Population and Census and Surveys.)*

Holland, Belgium and West Germany, all prosperous industrial countries, have more people per square mile than the UK. *(Pan World Atlas, 1973.)*

MYTH: Immigrants take British jobs.
FACT: During the 1950s and '60s, when there was a shortage of labour, like many industrialised countries we looked to other countries to help us out. Eleven per cent of the total work-forces in West Germany and France, and 28 per cent of that in Switzerland, are migrants, compared with 7.5 per cent of workers in Britain.

MYTH: Blacks come here to sponge off the state.
FACT: Blacks, here, are a younger group than whites, so proportionately more blacks than whites are working and therefore paying income tax and national insurance. Of black men, 91 per cent are working compared with 77 per cent of white men.

Since there are proportionately fewer older people in the black community, they take less from the state than the white population.

MYTH: The black population of this country is many millions.
FACT: The latest estimate (mid-1976) of the size of the black population is 1¾ million – 3.3 per cent of the total population. In 1974 nearly 40 per cent of the black people had been born in Great Britain and therefore were not immigrants.

MYTH: Because they don't speak English they hold back our children at school.
FACT: Many children of immigrant parents were born here and English is their first language.

Most local education authorities make arrangements to teach English to non-English-speaking children in special classes with special teachers so that they do not impede the progress of the rest of the children.

There is no evidence that the proportion of black children in a class has any significant influence on the attainment of white pupils. *(Language Proficiency in the Multi-Racial Junior School: A Comparative Study, NFER, 1975; Race and Education across Cultures, Heinemann, 1975.)*

MYTH: Immigrants are running down British inner-city areas.
FACT: Urban decay has existed in this country since the Industrial Revolution. Bad housing conditions were here long before black immigrants. In the areas where 70 per cent of black people live, eight out of ten people are white. *(Census 1971.)*

Crossword clues

ACROSS

1. Three points to view (3)
2. Mixed up ruse is certain (4)
4. Also, instrument without novice (3)
6. London to Cambridge for £50 in trip offer – is this a bargain? (3-3)
8. Usually has a limited following (2)
9. Preposition found in Oslo, Norway (2)
11. Property baron takes rent (8)
15. Meadow from mixed-up ale (3)
16. Night-club act (7)
18. Lucifer likes it like this (3)
19. Shorter than father (3)
21. Competent, but not totally capable (4)
23. Old-fashioned promise (6)
24. A short connection (2)

DOWN

1. Good man takes a turn to walk (6)
2. Gentle in lots of touches (4)
3. Unusual care is needed for this contest (4)
4. A spinning summit (3)
5. Frequently loses ten for genitive pronoun (2)
7. At home (2)
10. Mate without point is cooked (5)
12. Even a teetotaller would get a hangover from this (7)
13. A tidy whisky – without water (4)
14. Pat bad back (3)
17. Money given to treasury – it strains (5)
20. It's indiscreet to let the cat out of this (3)
22. To exist from beer with no queen (2)

DIA(----)MAR *Can you find a word which completes the first word and begins the second?*

With 12 matches make 6 triangles;
with 12 matches make 14 triangles.

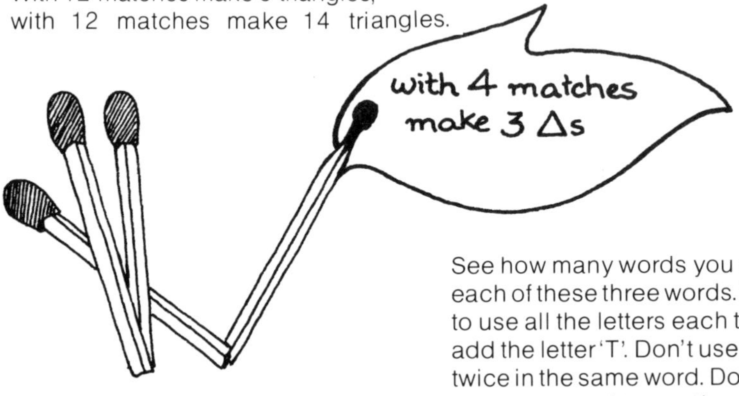

See how many words you can make from each of these three words. You don't have to use all the letters each time but always add the letter 'T'. Don't use the same letter twice in the same word. Don't move letters from one word to another.

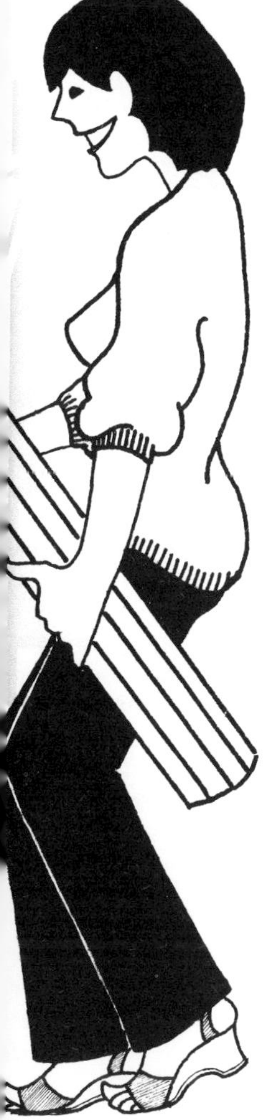

Shown here is a highly diagrammatic map of mainland Europe. The countries are indicated by abbreviations, which should help you to identify them. (If not, there's always an atlas.)

Travelling only overland, can you visit all of the countries on the map once and only once?

If it is not possible to visit all of the countries as described above, what is the greatest number of countries that can be visited once and only once?

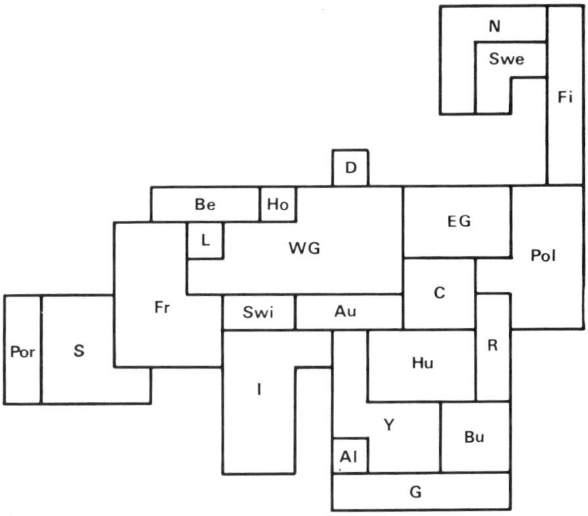

Three dead men were found in a special room. There was one gun, one used bullet and one of the men was shot. How did the other two die and where were they?

ost on the moon problem sheet

›u are in a space-crew orig- ılly scheduled to rendezvous ›h a mother-ship on the lighted ›rface of the moon. Mech- ›ical difficulties, however, ›ve forced your ship to crash- ›d at a spot some 200 miles ›m the rendezvous point.

The rough landing damaged ›ch of the equipment aboard. ›ce survival depends on ›aching the mother-ship, the ›st critical items available ›st be chosen for the 200- ›le trip.

Below are listed the 15 items left intact after landing. Your task is to rank them in terms of their importance to your crew in its attempt to reach the rendezvous-point. Place the number **1** by the most important item, number **2** by the second-most important, and so on to number **15**, the least important.

..... Box of matches
..... Food concentrate
..... 50 feet of nylon rope
..... Parachute silk
..... Portable heating unit
..... Two .45 caliber pistols
..... One case dehydrated milk
..... Two 100-pound tanks of oxygen
..... Stellar map (of the moon's constellation)
..... Life-raft
..... Magnetic compass
..... Five gallons of water
..... Signal flares
..... First-aid kit containing injection needles
..... Solar-powered receiver-transmitter

A TASTE OF BRITAIN

Fast food

In the past ten years or so, America's most popular export to Britain has been THE HAMBURGER. One very well-known American company which has restaurants all over the world even has its own "university". Here, if you fancy becoming an expert in the subject, you can take a ten-day course leading to the "degree" Batchelor of Hamburgerology. If you get really interested in the subject, you can even go on to do your Master's degree – but that takes longer!

Hamburgers are, of course, fast food: they don't take long to cook and they take even less time to eat. The ideology of fast-food restaurants centres on the time it takes to get the customer in and out of the building.

Next time you're in one of them, look around. You'll notice that they aren't usually very comfortable (they don't want to encourage you to hang around for too long). And they're normally decorated in bright, garish colours because pyschological tests are supposed to show that this makes people hungrier. The chips – oops, sorry, we mean French Fries – have a rather peculiar texture. This is because they're made from granules of dried potato which are put into a machine, mixed with water, then squeezed out of a square tube so that they resemble real French Fries.

Thirsty? Why not try a milk-style shake. Again, don't expect to get real milk...why bother with the real thing when you can buy milk powder which doesn't go off, and when added to water makes almost the real thing?

Keen students of English should read the menus in these places. If you think you could do with improving your vocabulary, especially adjectives, study them with care.

Eat, drink and be merry

A lot of countries now have very strict laws about drinking and driving. In Britain, for example, the legal limit for alcohol in the bloodstream when driving is 80mg. of alcohol per 100ml. of blood. In other words, if you drink more than about two pints of beer, you shouldn't be driving.

Of course, the effect of the same amount of alcohol on people of different ages and weights varies quite a lot. And if you drink on an empty stomach, the effect will be much quicker because the alcohol is more easily absorbed into the bloodstream.

If you are stopped by the police and suspected of being drunk, they will breathalyse you. This involves blowing into a bag containing clear crystals. If they turn green this shows, roughly, that you could be over the limit and you will be asked to go to the police station for a further test.

If this proves positive, you will be prosecuted. On conviction, disqualification from driving for a year is normally automatic, together with a fine of up to £400 and/or imprisonment for up to two years.

The two-pints-of-beer limit is well-known, but people often forget the alcoholic content of other drinks. Foreign visitors are often confused by our eccentric way of measuring drinks. What do you think is the alcoholic content of the drinks at the top of the page compared with a pint of beer? Left to right, they are: a large glass of scotch, two glasses of sherry, two glasses of wine and two thirds of a pint of cider.

Knickerbocker Glory **60p**

A long luscious combination of strawberries, fruit cocktail and ice cream – the summit sprinkled with chocolate vermicelli.

Banana Long Boat **60p**

A whole banana, split lengthwise, with fruit cocktail and a jumbo-size portion of ice cream topped with chocolate vermicelli.

A computer flowchart

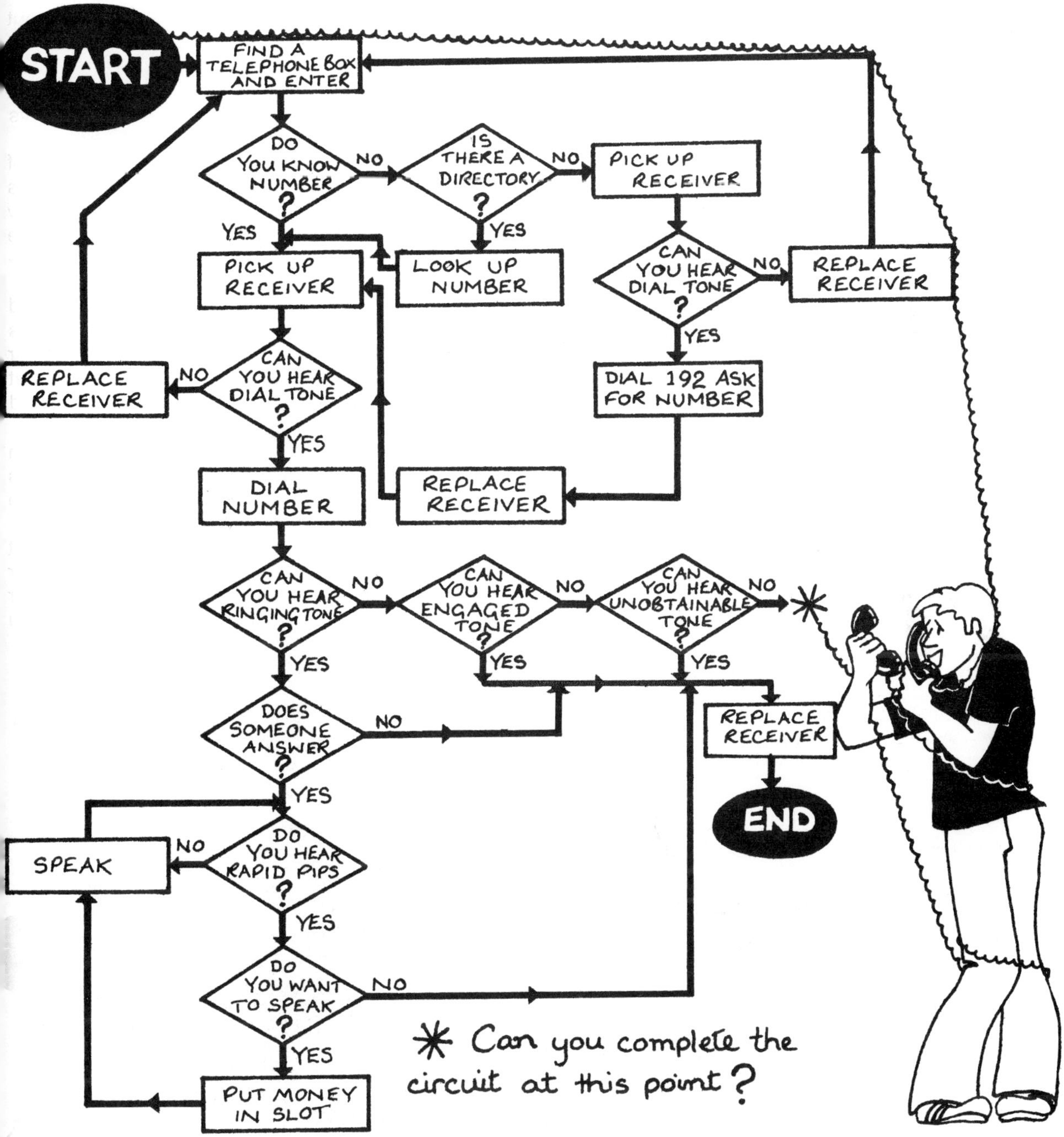

* Can you complete the circuit at this point?

A shopping walk

1

2

3

4

Each of these comments goes with a photo – can you match them up?

a) I'm glad it's not your birthday every day of the week. Now make up your mind – what are you going to get?

b) I wonder what we'll get for it? I couldn't believe it when they said it was so old!

c) It's just over a pound but I'll only charge you 15p, love.

d) Round and round, every hour on the hour – it's enough to make you dizzy!

e) People don't usually see me, but I always see them. I've got such a good view from up here.

f) There's never a dull moment working round here, there's always somebody up to something.

g) Gee, what a lovely old fashioned store!

h) Looking at it now – you'd never believe it, would you?

6

7

5

8

Alternative ideas

The school day at the White Lion School, Islington, North London.

The White Lion school was set up as an alternative to State education; it is called a "free school" because the children are not forced to conform to any adult's definition of discipline or learning. They are free to choose what and how they want to learn.

The school opens when the first child arrives, usually at 8.45 am, but the children can arrive when they like. Most of them are in school by ten. Between nine and ten most people are in the living-room and the kitchen downstairs. Many of the children haven't had much breakfast so there is a lot of tea-drinking and toast-making and talking. This is a time when children and adults can work out what they are to do for the day.

By about ten most of the children are busily doing something but not every child will want to be involved immediately. Some of them will want to play and others will sit and read the papers.

On a typical morning in June two children were in the living-room, an adult was making the lunch and a parent was in the office answering the phone. Two children had just arrived and were talking on the stairs. Two were icing cakes in the nursery.

In the pottery-room, one of the older girls was finishing off a pot. Some children were in the maths-and-science room making model aeroplanes. Six children were upstairs; two were working on a project concerning their flats and the others were reading and drawing. Four of the older boys were on their way to Hornchurch Cardrome for driving lessons.

During the morning one adult, usually helped by several children, makes the lunch. There is a rota-system for jobs like this so that everyone gets a chance to do the lunch about once a week. Lunch is served at around one o'clock and is eaten in the living room. After lunch it is someone else's turn to do the washing-up. This is a very unpopular job and most of the children are reluctant to help. As the adults are also reluctant to do it on their own, they usually reach a compromise. After lunch, the children carry on with their activities until 4.30.

On Mondays, Tuesdays and Thursdays the school is open in the evenings until 9 pm. The same kind of activities continue during the evenings. On Tuesday evening the school is also open to visitors between 7 and 9 pm. On Wednesday afternoon and evening there is a school meeting. On Friday there is no evening school but occasionally there is an outside activity planned, such as a visit to the cinema. The school is also open every weekend.

About time

In my lifetime
Time and time again
People have said:
"Don't waste time
Don't get out of time
Stay in time
Get there on time
Don't be small-time
Hit the big time"

Timely advice
To a time-waster
Like me
In the meantime
Killing time
Takes up all of my time

They say: "Time flies
When you're having fun"
In my case
Finding spare time
Is a question of timing

In no time
I'll be saying:
"Why did I waste time?
Why did I take so much time off?"
Time's funny
It's never here
It's either coming or it's gone

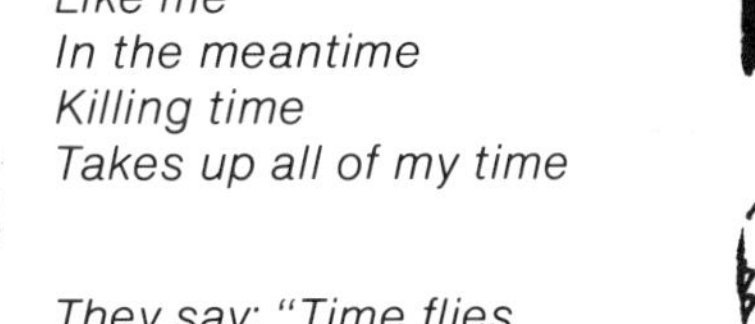

Brass rubbing

A rubbing is made by placing a piece of paper over a metal or stone object that has indentations. Wax is then rubbed over the paper until an image of the object shows on it. The rubbing can then be framed and put on a wall like a picture. Why not try making one and taking it home as a present?

All you need is some white lining-paper, which you can buy from a wallpaper shop, and wax. Heel-ball wax is the best and you can get it from most shoe-repair shops. It comes in sticks, best for delicate objects, or cakes, fine for bigger rubbings.

The most popular types of rubbings are of brass memorial stones which were used to cover graves. They are usually likenesses of the dead person and were most popular from the 13th to the 15th Centuries. You can find them in old churches, but because of the damage that could be caused by enthusiastic but inexperienced rubbers, many vicars now refuse permission for them to be rubbed. In order to preserve existing brasses, yet still encourage rubbing, centres around Britain have been set up where you can go and learn how to do it by using reproduction brasses.

If you don't feel like starting with something as big as a church brass, look around the streets of any town. There are all kinds of interesting objects that make lovely rubbings.

Some people enjoy rubbing coal-hole covers! Most of these were made in the mid-19th Century. They were designed to fit into the road and cover up the holes leading to the cellars where coal was stored. When a family needed more coal, the cover was lifted up and the coal was poured directly into the cellar below. If you look at the covers closely, you'll see they have an amazing variety of designs: stars, crosses, circles, squares and even snowflakes.

Post-boxes are good too. They all have on them the initials (called ciphers) of the reigning monarch of the time they were made, so you can get interesting historical rubbings from them.

There are a lot of different ways to get your rubbing but the easiest is just to put your piece of white paper over the object (make sure this is clean by rubbing it first with a cloth), fix it with tape or weight it down with books. Then start to rub hard with the wax. Always rub in the same direction. Take your time and rub only in sections. Don't worry if you go over the edges, most rubbings are cut out and then stuck on to a thicker piece of paper or card.

When you've finished, take a piece of nylon (old tights are good) and polish the surface of the rubbing until the wax shines. White paper and black wax produce a negative image. A positive one is easy to make too – use white paper and ordinary white candle wax. Rub in the way described above and polish with nylon. When you get home, lie the rubbing flat and weight the edges. Then soak a sponge in water, squeeze out and dip into a saucer of black Indian ink. Quickly and lightly go over the rubbing with this. As the ink penetrates the unwaxed parts it will fill in as a dark background leaving an ivory coloured object. Wipe off excess ink with a tissue and leave it to dry.

Roll up your rubbings carefully and put them into cardboard tubes so that you can carry them home safely and mount them there.

Impression of a finished brass rubbing. The original version was several feet high.